Lester

OTHER BOOKS BY YVES ENGLER

Playing Left Wing — From Rink Rat to Student Radical

Canada in Haiti — Waging War on the Poor Majority (With Anthony Fenton)

The Black Book of Canadian Foreign Policy

Canada and Israel — Building Apartheid

Stop Signs — Cars and Capitalism on the Road to Economic, Social, and Ecological Decay (With Bianca Mugyenyi)

Lester Pearson's Peacekeeping

— The Truth May Hurt

Yves Engler

RED Publishing/Fernwood Publishing

2012

Copyright © 2012 Yves Engler
All rights reserved. No part of this book may be reproduced or transmitted
in any form by any means without permission in writing from the publisher,
except by a reviewer, who may quote brief passages in a review.
First printing March 2012
Cover by Working Design
Printed and bound in Canada by Transcontinental Printing
A co-publication of
RED Publishing
2736 Cambridge Street, Vancouver, British Columbia V5K 1L7 and
Fernwood Publishing
32 Oceanvista Lane, Black Point, Nova Scotia B0J 1B0
and 748 Broadway Avenue, Winnipeg, Manitoba, R3G 0X3
www.fernwoodpublishing.ca

Fernwood Publishing Company Limited gratefully acknowledges the
financial support of the Government of Canada through the Canada Book
Fund and the Canada Council for the Arts, the Nova Scotia Department of
Communities, Culture and Heritage, the Manitoba Department of Culture,
Heritage and Tourism under the Manitoba Publishers Marketing Assistance
Program and the Province of Manitoba, through the Book Publishing Tax
Credit, for our publishing program.

Library and Archives Canada Cataloguing in Publication
Lester Pearson's peacekeeping : the truth may hurt / Yves Engler
Includes bibliographical references.

ISBN 978-1-55266-510-7

1. Pearson, Lester B., 1897-1972. 2. Canada--Foreign relations--
1945-. 3. Canada--Foreign relations--United States. 4. United States--
Foreign relations--Canada. 5. Canada--Politics and government--1963-1968.
6. Prime ministers--Canada--Biography. I.Title.

FC621.P4E54 2012   971.064'3092   C2011-908419-8

Contents

Chronology 7
Foreword by Noam Chomsky 8
Introduction: A Great Canadian Loved by All 13
1. Early Years 18
2. Aligning Canada with US Interests 25
3. Minister for Fighting Asian Nationalism 46
4. A Commitment to Democracy? 74
5. Riding the Atom Bomb to the Prime Minister's Office . 92
6. Prime Minister Pearson and Colonialism 100
7. The Case for War Crime Charges 117
8. Conclusion — Leading by Deferring to Power 135
Bibliography 152
Endnotes 163

Lester Pearson Chronology

1897 Born
1913 Enrolls at the University of Toronto
1928 Begins working at External Affairs
1935 Assistant to High Commissioner in London
1941 Assistant Undersecretary of External Affairs
1942 Envoy Extraordinaire to US embassy
1945 US ambassador
1946 Undersecretary of External Affairs
1948 External Affairs Minister
1958 Leader of the Official Opposition
1963 Prime Minister
1968 Retired from politics
1969 Chancellor Carleton University
1972 Died

Foreword
By Noam Chomsky

Unlike the US during speaking trips in Canada major media would interview me. But, the discussion would invariably concern US foreign-policy. Tired of focusing on the US, I decided to talk about Canada, which changed the reception.

The first time was on CBC radio's Morningside with long-time host Peter Gzowski. When I spoke in Toronto, Morningside would invite me on and Gzowski asked leading questions about US foreign-policy. He seemed happy to hear criticism of the US. One time I decided to talk about Canada. After a question about flying in I said, "I landed at war criminal airport". He said: "What do you mean?" I responded, "the Lester B. Pearson Airport". Gzowski replied "war criminal?" So I detailed Pearson's support for the war in Vietnam: the spying, weapons sales and complicity in the bombing of the North.

Gzowski was infuriated. He went into a tantrum, haranguing me for a number of minutes. To me Gzowski's reaction was sort of funny but apparently his listeners were angry that he was impolite. When leaving, the producer stopped me and said "oh my god, the switchboards are lighting up, we're getting thousands of phone calls from across the country". Morningside's producer was so embarrassed they did a follow-up interview from Boston in which Gzowski made sure to be polite, though they never asked me to be on the show again.

***

Canada's Nobel Peace Prize winner and eminent statesman, Lester Pearson was a major criminal, really extreme. He didn't have the power to be like an American president, but if he'd had it, he would have been the same. He tried.

Reflecting a hardline Cold War doctrine, in 1953 Pearson declared in the House of Commons that, "it is becoming increasingly clear from the events in Indochina that there is a strategic connection between communist aggression in one part of the world and communist aggression in another." What concerned Pearson particularly was the aggression then being conducted by the Vietnamese against the French in Vietnam. As he had explained two years earlier before the House: "if the valiant efforts now being made by France to defend and complete the independence of Indochina were to fail, all of southeast Asia, including Burma, Malaya and Indonesia, with their important resources of rubber, rice and tin, might well come under communist control," with repercussions throughout South Asia.

This conception is one found in US documents of the period. Pearson's view was that "Soviet colonial authority in Indochina would appear to be stronger than that of France" — this at a time when major French military forces were attempting to regain control of their former colony and no Russians were in sight. Both the US and Canada recognized, ruefully, that Ho Chi Minh and his Vietnamese resistance had overwhelming domestic support in the struggle against the US-backed French invaders, and that the puppet regimes established by France had no legitimacy. But no matter: Ho Chi Minh was just an agent of Russian colonialism and aggression. The Indochina "hotspot" was the fault of the Russians, in absentia.

The US-French invasion, backed by Canada, came close to nuclear war. The US was planning direct intervention at the time of the Dien Bien Phu battle. The chairman of the Joint Chiefs of Staff advised that the use of tactical nuclear weapons could be "the best means of smashing [the Viet Minh] and cleaning up Indochina." Secretary of State John Foster Dulles stated that "in case of an all out Viet Minh attack," there would probably be "general war with China." "Our concept," he continued, "envisages a fight with nuclear weapons rather than a commitment to ground forces." This was October 1954. Dulles was concerned about a possible Viet Minh response to American actions to subvert the Geneva peace agreements and to continue the war against Vietnam.

A few months earlier, in August, the National Security Council had established a doctrine that was to be reiterated year after year: in the event of "local communist subversion or rebellion not constituting armed attack" — specifically, popular resistance to US backed terrorism in South Vietnam in violation of the Geneva Accords — the US would consider intervening directly with military force, also attacking China if this seemed "necessary and feasible." These crucial documents (NSC-5429/2 and others), which express a clear and explicit commitment to violate international law, are invariably suppressed in academic and popular histories. The standard account is the Pearson version of the Party Line: France — and consequently the United States — were defending Vietnam against Vietnamese aggression.

Canada continued to adhere to what John Holmes, the influential Canadian diplomat and Pearson confidant, called "the

Canadian idea": "You hang on to your principles but you find a way around [them]." James Eayrs documents that, as a member of the International Control Commission (ICC), Canada routinely passed on military information to Washington, though Pearson was concerned that this be kept secret to avoid "very serious repercussions" (i.e., damage to Canada's image). The editor of the Montréal Star later wrote that the Canadians in the ICC "are functioning as spies when they were supposed to be serving as international civil servants."

In 1964 Pearson was informed by President Lyndon Johnson about US plans to bomb North Vietnam the following year. His reaction was positive, though according to McGeorge Bundy's notes, he expressed "great reservations about the use of nuclear weapons" — caution befitting a Nobel Peace Prize Laureate. As the American war against Indochina escalated, Canada participated enthusiastically, selling over $500 million worth of military equipment to the US, so that by 1970, it was, per capita, the largest international arms exporter. One Canadian commentator, George Grant, wrote that behind the high-minded rhetoric, Canadian society had become "a machine for greed, and our branch plant industry is making a packet out of the demolition of Vietnam." In a study published by the Canadian University Press Service, Ian Wiseman wrote that "every university in Canada received money from the US Defense complex" — meanwhile upholding "the Canadian idea."

***

In every country the powerful attempt to define history. Yves Engler's books — *The Black Book of Canadian Foreign Policy*, *Canada and Israel: Building Apartheid* and *Lester Pearson's Peacekeeping: The Truth May Hurt* — provide an important counterweight to the dominant understanding of Canada's role in the world, posing a challenge to citizens willing to take their fundamental responsibilities seriously.

Introduction:
A Great Canadian Loved by All

More than a political biography, this book is part of a larger attempt to rethink Canada's role in the world. To do so, one must seek the truth regardless of myths destroyed or popular illusions shattered. Without an honest accounting of our foreign policy past, how can we expect to change course and create a better future?

The only Canadian to win the Nobel Peace Prize, Lester Bowles "Mike" Pearson has been called "Canada's greatest diplomat".[1] More than anyone he symbolizes a benevolent Canadian foreign policy and the idea that this country has been an "honest broker" in international affairs.

As a result, Pearson is lionized across the country. There is a road, college, peace-park, civic centre, housing project and an international airport named in his honour. Québec's largest English-language school board and schools in almost every province are dedicated to a politician who lost two elections as Liberal leader and never won a majority government. Involved in formulating Canadian foreign policy for four decades, many international affairs institutions celebrate Pearson. His name appears on the Ottawa-based Pearson Peacekeeping Centre while the United Nations Association in Canada bequeaths a Pearson Medal of Peace for an individual's "contribution to international service". Most significantly, the Department of Foreign Affairs and International Trade is housed in Ottawa's Lester B. Pearson Building.

Forty years after his death the former external affairs minister still features regularly in foreign policy debates. In September 2009 Liberal leader Michael Ignatieff said his government would "take global leadership that has made Canada's reputation since the time of Lester B. Pearson. ... A Canada that inspires, leads the world by example, and makes us all proud."[2] A few months later the head of the Greens, Elizabeth May, claimed "a Green Party approach to international issues will return Canada to the values of Lester B. Pearson." For his part, the late NDP leader Jack Layton dropped his name during a June 2010 House of Commons debate. "Recently, we had the UN special advisor, Jeffrey Sachs, slamming our Minister and saying that Canada was failing to live up to the tradition of Lester Pearson by falling far short of his target for international aid."[3]

It's not only politicians who sing his praise; many leftwing commentators echo this view. In a May 2008 *Toronto Star* column titled "Keep Pearson out of it" Linda McQuaig took exception with "[former Liberal minister] John Manley, head of the government's advisory panel on Afghanistan, defend[ing] the mission by invoking the name of Canadian peacekeeping hero Lester Pearson." Author of a 2007 book that covered his foreign policy, McQuaig quoted an academic who called this a "real desecration of [Pearson's] memory and his monumental achievement for world peace."

Lester Pearson's Peacekeeping

The president of the Rideau Institute, Ottawa's most left-wing foreign policy think tank, has made similar statements. Steven Staples co-authored a 2008 article explaining "Pearson's vision of the Canadian military supporting the United Nations in negotiating solutions has been replaced by an Americanized vision of militaristic solutions imposed by the force of arms."[4] Left wing author Naomi Klein also dabbled in the mythmaking. In a 2000 *Globe and Mail* piece she referred to a Liberal Party campaign focused on "Lester Pearson's legacy of international compassion."[5]

Myths are often closely held, becoming part of one's identity. As part of the promotion for my *Black Book of Canadian Foreign Policy* I put together a press release titled The Top 10 Things You Don't Know About Canadian Foreign Policy. Number 1 was "Many commentators, including the world's leading intellectual, Noam Chomsky, consider Lester Pearson a war criminal." I sent the list and offered a review copy to a reporter at *Embassy*, Canada's leading foreign policy newsletter. He responded with outrage: "Frankly, I'm not that interested in Chomsky's opinions, especially when they smear great Canadians like Mike Pearson. I know you're a radical, but have some pride in Canada!"

This book is a response to the deification of Lester Pearson that takes place across the political spectrum. It challenges the widely held view of Pearson as a peace promoting and altruistic diplomat/politician. There is, in fact, a strong case to be made that he should be posthumously charged with abetting war crimes.

How do we make that case and by what standards should we judge Pearson's foreign policy? In the *Black Book of Canadian Foreign Policy* this standard is offered: "I believe Earth is our home and we are its stewards. While citizens of Canada, we are also neighbours to everyone who shares this planet. We must be good neighbours. That should be the underlying premise of Canada's foreign policy." While this is a good starting point, we can also reference the following set of principles that Pearson had a hand in creating, the United Nations Charter:

> *WE THE PEOPLES OF THE UNITED NATIONS DETERMINED*
>
> *to save succeeding generations from the scourge of war, which twice in our lifetime has brought untold sorrow to mankind, and*
>
> *to reaffirm faith in fundamental human rights, in the dignity and worth of the human person, in the equal rights of men and women and of nations large and small, and*
>
> *to establish conditions under which justice and respect for the obligations arising from treaties and other sources of international law can be maintained, and*
>
> *to promote social progress and better standards of life in larger freedom,*
>
> *AND FOR THESE ENDS*
>
> *to practice tolerance and live together in peace with one another as good neighbours, and*
>
> *to unite our strength to maintain international peace and security, and*
>
> *to ensure, by the acceptance of principles and the institution of methods, that armed force shall not be used, save in the common interest, and*
>
> *to employ international machinery for the promotion of the economic and social advancement of all peoples,*
>
> *HAVE RESOLVED TO COMBINE OUR EFFORTS TO ACCOMPLISH THESE AIMS*

> *Accordingly, our respective Governments, through representatives assembled in the city of San Francisco, who have exhibited their full powers found to be in good and due form, have agreed to the present Charter of the United Nations and do hereby establish an international organization to be known as the United Nations.*

This is a standard to which we can fairly hold Pearson's foreign policy accountable. If a truth and reconciliation commission about Canada's foreign policy past were held, adherence to the UN Charter would certainly be part of the criteria by which actions would be judged.

In writing this book the author has imagined himself gathering material for such a truth and reconciliation commission. The reader is asked to imagine her/himself as a member of the commission. It's your job to study the evidence before deciding how best to characterize Lester Bowles "Mike" Pearson. Was he a great diplomat? Going forward, should this country emulate "his" foreign policy? What lessons can be learned from his life and times?

1. Early Years

In 1897 Pearson was born into the "establishment" but it was not necessarily a background "of money but of education and upbringing."[1] His father and one grandfather were prominent Methodist ministers in southern Ontario. White, Anglo-Saxon and Protestant Pearson was taught to support British imperialism. During the 1898-1902 Boer War the future diplomat's father called on his parishioners to stand with England and at a young age Mike was exposed to imperialist author Rudyard Kipling (of White Man's Burden fame).[2] As a young man Pearson "naturally shared [UK Prime Minister] Lloyd George's affection and respect for the Empire," explains John A. English in *Shadow of Heaven*. "Mike's imperialism derived from a liberal belief in the beneficence and generosity of British rule."[3]

In 1913 a sixteen year-old Pearson enrolled at the University of Toronto's Victoria College where his cousin was chancellor. Two years later he left U of T's Methodist College to fight in Europe's first Great War. He joined the Canadian Army Medical Corps, working as a stretcher-bearer in a Greek hospital. Unhappy with his situation in Greece, Mike asked his Dad to pull some strings. *Pearson: Unlikely Gladiator* explains: "Through family connections to the Minister of Militia and Defense, Sir Sam

Hughes, he wangled a transfer to officer training in England and then to a pilot's course with the Royal Flying Corps."[4]

Pearson celebrated one of the most absurd and destructive wars in history. Fifteen million people were killed and another 20 million wounded in this conflict between rising imperial power Germany and leading colonial powers England and France. With both sides entrenched, the western front of the war barely moved from September 1914 to July 1917. Millions of young men lost their lives fighting over a few kilometers of territory. Among them were nearly 60,000 Canadian soldiers. Another 150,000 were wounded.

In August 1917 Robert Borden's government passed the Military Service Act. The conscription of young men sparked widespread dissent, particularly in Quebéc. During the Conscription Crisis a 20 year-old Mike described "opponents of conscription as treasonous, 'detestable... [giving Canada] a bad name.'"[5] Five decades later he called World War I "the battlefield on which we became nationally conscious and proud of our Canadian identity."[6]

Given a year's credit for service overseas Pearson returned to finish his final year at the University of Toronto. After graduating he joined a large Chicago-based meatpacking company where his uncle was a senior executive. Pearson worked with the company for a short period in Hamilton and then moved to Chicago. He didn't like the work so Pearson returned to school with help from his former dean of residence at Victoria College. Vincent Massey (from one of Toronto's wealthiest families) secured the future diplomat a Massey Foundation Fellowship.

After two years at the University of Oxford Pearson was recruited by the University of Toronto's dean of history, George Wrong, a close friend of Massey.[7] Pearson taught there for four years, marrying his student, Maryon Elspeth Moody, along the way. A popular teacher, he was not particularly interested in research. Under increasing pressure to publish he jumped at the opportunity to join the newly created External Affairs Department. A former University of Toronto colleague, Hume Wrong, recommended Pearson to the external affairs undersecretary in 1927 and over the next seven years he worked on various government files, including the Royal Commission on Price Spreads, the League of Nations and a London naval conference. The hard-working and able diplomat was moving up in the world. In 1935 Pearson was posted to London where he became an assistant to Canadian High Commissioner Vincent Massey.

On the most important issue of the day — the rising tide of fascism — Pearson's thinking largely reflected the English and Canadian elite. In 1922 Benito Mussolini came to power backed by wealth-holders and a Vatican worried about the growth of Italy's Left five years after the Russian revolution. To the north of Italy, Adolf Hitler took power in 1933. As the Nazis consolidated their control they repressed Germany's Left and implemented a series of anti-Semitic laws. At the same time Hitler vociferously denounced the Bolsheviks in Russia. Pearson was ambivalent towards the fascists, though he had limited influence on Canadian policy. As late as May 1937 he demonstrated little concern regarding the Nazi's treatment of Jews or their repression of the Left.[8] Nor was Pearson bothered by Germany's arms buildup or their reoccupation of the Rhineland.[9] In a 2009 biography, Andrew Cohen notes "in his response to the Nazis — in private or public — he was slow, late and tepid."[10]

The struggle between fascism and liberal democracy was forcefully thrust upon the world stage in Spain. A left-wing coalition government won office there in 1936. The church, landed gentry and big business immediately looked to overthrow the Republican government with the help of General Francisco Franco, commander of Spain's overseas military. Hitler's Germany, Fascist Portugal and Mussolini's Italy sent large quantities of weapons and tens of thousands of troops to support Franco. With major British economic interests in that country, Canada effectively sided with the Fascists during the Spanish Civil War. Supposedly neutral Ottawa refused repeated requests from Spain's elected government to sell it weaponry and outlawed recruiting Canadians to fight against the rising tide of fascism.

Hitler and Mussolini were emboldened by their victory in Spain, which could have been averted if Canada, Britain and other leading capitalist countries had backed the Republican forces. A different outcome in Spain may have saved Europe from the incredible destruction of World War II, which probably embarrassed Pearson. This could be why Mike largely ignored the Spanish Civil War in his three volume *Memoirs* despite having been close to the action as a diplomat in England.[11]

After Undersecretary O.D. Skelton died in 1941 Pearson left London to become Assistant Undersecretary of External Affairs. His stint in this position was short-lived. Ten months later he became a special envoy to Washington, which became the centre of military planning after the US entered World War II. Pearson quickly developed close ties to American officials. On one occasion a friend at the White House asked him to ghost write a letter for President Franklin Delano Roosevelt congratulating Prime Minister Mackenzie King on the third anniversary of the British Commonwealth's air training plan.[12] On January 1, 1945 Pearson became Canada's ambassador in Washington, one of the country's most important diplomatic positions. Close to US planning circles when they decided to drop nuclear bombs on Hiroshima and Nagasaki in August 1945, his views on these events are unclear. He said little in his *Memoirs*[13] even though Canada spent millions of dollars (tens of millions in 2012 money) to help research the bombs' development.[14] Immediately after successfully developing the technology, the US submitted its proposal to drop the bomb on Japan to the tri-state World War II Combined Policy Committee meeting, which included powerful Canadian minister C.D. Howe and a British official.[15] Though there is no record of his comments at the July 4, 1945 meeting, apparently Howe supported the US proposal. Canada also contributed uranium for the bomb. One author noted "the maiming of Hiroshima and Nagasaki was a byproduct of Canadian uranium."[16] (Reflecting the racism in Canadian governing circles, in his (uncensored) diary Mackenzie King wrote: "It is fortunate that the use of the bomb should have been upon the Japanese rather than upon the white races of Europe."[17])

Three months before the US nuked Japan, Ambassador Pearson and Undersecretary Norman Robertson represented Canada at the founding of the United Nations in California. At the San Francisco conference, notes *The Middle Power Project*, "Pearson took the lead [within the Canadian delegation], arguing that Canada had best not vote against the great powers, particularly not against less crucial Anglo-American proposals."[18] He ignored the leader of the Co-operative Commonwealth Federation (the NDP's predecessor), M.J. Coldwell, who said Canada shouldn't be overly concerned with Washington and Moscow's position. Pearson also opposed Australian Foreign Minister Herbert Evatt's campaign to check the power of the strongest countries. "After one of Evatt's many outbursts against the United States, Great Britain, and the Soviet Union, Pearson personally intervened to try to defuse tensions," notes *Parties Long Estranged*.[19] He "puzzled at his [Evatt's] apparent lack of concern over some of the plain facts of world politics."[20] Canada's ambassador to Washington accepted the idea that the most powerful, particularly the US, should rule the new international organization. During a break in negotiations Pearson told a Los Angeles conference: "We agree that power and responsibility should be related, that absolute equality in any world organization would mean absolute futility. No country will be able to play its proper part in international affairs if its influence there bears no adequate relation to its obligations and its power."[21] In other words, the UN should solidify the status quo, not democratize it.

    The Prime Minister of New Zealand called the veto for major powers "an evil thing" while the Australian officials in San Francisco pushed a proposal without a veto for permanent members of the Security Council.[22] In a move with long-lasting implications the Canadian delegation abstained on this Australian motion, denying them the single vote needed to carry the meeting. After this close vote Pearson is said to have asked the US delegation whether it would sign the new international organization's charter without the veto.[23] They said no, prompting Ottawa to declare its support for the permanent Security Council members' veto. "Canada Switches to Back Big 5 Veto," blared the front page of the *New York Times*.[24] Probably the most important middle power at the time, five medium and smaller countries followed Ottawa's lead.[25] But, the poorer and smaller countries subsequently picked Australia, not Canada, to sit on the opening incarnation of the Security Council.

Lester Pearson's Peacekeeping

In September 1946 Pearson returned to Ottawa to become Undersecretary of External Affairs. The *New York Times* praised Pearson's four-year stint in the US capital. "He won the respect, confidence, and affection of a remarkably wide range of persons in most phases of Washington life."[26]

Pearson led the External Affairs bureaucracy for two years. From this position he played an important role in creating the North Atlantic Treaty Organization (NATO) and influenced the UN negotiations on the British mandate of Palestine. Prior to winning a seat in the House of Commons, Pearson was appointed Minister of External Affairs. From September 1948 to June 1957 Prime Minister Louis St. Laurent's Liberal Cabinet gave Pearson a broad mandate to direct this country's foreign policy. As minister he pushed to send Canadian troops to Korea and helped resolve the Suez Crisis.

In 1958 he was chosen Liberal leader and between then and 1963 Pearson had much less influence over Canadian foreign policy as leader of the official opposition. As prime minister from 1963 to 1968 Pearson once again oversaw this country's international policy. During that time he backed Israel during the Six Day War and provided substantial support to the US war in Indochina.

The following chapters will go into detail about Pearson's role in specific aspects of Canadian foreign policy.

2. Aligning Canada with US Interests

An important player in determining Canada's foreign affairs by the end of World War II, the Cold War was Pearson's first major test as a Canadian diplomat. His positions circumscribed subsequent policy.

In *Holding the Bully's Coat* Linda McQuaig claims Pearson had a "keenness to reduce Cold War tension with Moscow and Beijing."[1] There's little basis for this statement and a great deal of evidence to suggest the Nobel Peace Prize winner was a determined cold warrior. Before making his famous Iron Curtain speech, which some consider the opening salvo in the Cold War, former British Prime Minister, Winston Churchill, asked Canada's ambassador to Washington to look it over. Calling the March 1946 talk "one of the most impressive things that Churchill has done", Pearson made a correction and added a line he thought would be popular with the Missouri audience.[2]

This was one of Pearson's many contributions to Cold War hysteria. In an attempt to convince Prime Minister Mackenzie King to take a more strident position, the newly appointed undersecretary argued in a 1946 memo: "Without some fundamental change in the Soviet state system and the policies and views of its leaders, the USSR is ultimately bound to come into

25

open conflict with Western democracy."³ A year later Mike warned "the chief menace now is subversive aggressive communism, the servant of power politics."⁴

In a 1948 speech titled "Communism — the myth and reality" Pearson said the USSR was an "oppressor on a scale surpassing even Nazi Germany."⁵ He argued that the conflict between East and West was "spiritual" because "the crusading and subversive power of communism has been harnessed by a cold-blooded, calculating, victoriously powerful Slav empire."⁶

During his nine years as External Affairs Minister, Pearson repeatedly decried "communist imperialism" and "the international communist conspiracy" in the House of Commons.⁷ Before the House in early 1957 he referred to the "greatest colonial power of all and the one which exercises power in the most arbitrary and tyrannical fashion, the Soviet Union."⁸

Canada's contribution to the Cold War included the Canadian Psychological Warfare Committee, which continued after World War Two ended.⁹ As part of the Psychological Warfare Committee, the Canadian Broadcasting Corporation's International Service beamed Canadian information to the Soviet Union and other Eastern Bloc countries.¹⁰ In a 1951 speech to Parliament Pearson said CBC-IS was "playing a useful part in the psychological war against communism."¹¹ Viewing it as a "necessity" for government departments to have a "close liaison with the CBC international service", on July 1, 1952 Mike launched a Ukrainian section of CBC-IS.¹²

Established in 1949, NATO contributed to Cold War hysteria. Some believe NATO was a Canadian idea. Pearson began thinking about a formal western military alliance in 1946 and he laid out some of his thoughts on the topic in a June 1947 speech at the University of Rochester.[13] A few weeks later his assistant, Escott Reid, spoke (with Undersecretary Pearson's foreknowledge) in support "of collective self-defense against armed attack until the Security Council has acted."[14] In September of that year External Affairs Minister Louis St. Laurent told the UN General Assembly that if the Security Council remained "frozen in futility and divided by dissension" certain countries would "seek greater safety in an association of democratic and peace loving states willing to accept more specific international obligations in return for a greater measure of national security."[15] Pearson largely wrote this "first public proposal by a cabinet minister in the Atlantic area for an alliance for that region."[16] In March 1948 Undersecretary Pearson represented Canada at top-secret talks with Britain and the US on the possibility of creating a North Atlantic alliance.[17] He was also asked to be NATO's first secretary general.

Pearson wholeheartedly supported NATO. In his *Memoirs* he described the "formation of NATO" as the "most important thing I participated in".[18] *Canada and NATO* explains: "There would not again be, in Canada, the enthusiasm for the North Atlantic alliance there was in that close to 9 years that Louis St. Laurent stood behind it as the country's Prime Minister, and Lester Pearson as its Secretary of State for External Affairs."[19]

Pearson was not above red-baiting those who criticized NATO policy. When the Co-operative Commonwealth Federation (CCF) opposed a massive build-up of NATO troops in Europe in 1953, he claimed "the CCF seems to be moving towards that [Russian] position."[20] Pearson said the social democratic party's statement would "play straight into the hands of communist propaganda" and "that is exactly how the Kremlin would describe them."[21]

Lester Pearson's Peacekeeping

Officially, NATO was the West's response to an aggressive Soviet Union. But, the Cold War can be traced to Canada and its allies 1917 invasion of Russia, attempts to isolate that country throughout the 1920s and support for the Nazis anti-Bolshevik posture. To get a sense of Pearson's hostility toward Russia, in 1938 he said he hoped the Nazis and Soviets would destroy each other.

The idea that the US, or even Western Europe, was threatened by the Soviet Union after World War II is laughable. *NSC 68 and the Political Economy of the Early Cold War* notes: "At the end of the war, the Soviet Union lay in ruins virtually unimaginable to anyone who did not live through it. An estimated twenty-five million Soviet citizens and soldiers lost their lives fighting the invading Germans."[22] The US, on the other hand, came out of WWII much stronger than when they entered it. The continental US was untouched by fighting while the American economy benefited greatly from war production and exports.

After the destruction of WWII, the Soviets were not interested in fighting the US and its allies. This information was available to Pearson. In April 1945 Canada's ambassador to Russia, Dana Wilgress, concluded that "the interests of the Soviet privileged class are bound up with the maintenance of a long period of peace." The Soviet elite, the ambassador continued in an internal memo, was "fearful of the possibility of attack from abroad" and "obsessed with problems of security."[23] Wilgress believed the Soviets wanted a post-war alliance with the UK to guarantee peace in Europe (with a Soviet sphere in the East and a UK-led West.) Internally, US officials came to similar conclusions. Noam Chomsky notes the first supreme commander of NATO, Dwight Eisenhower's "consistent view that the Russians intended no military conquest of Western Europe."[24] A May 1949 US Department of Eastern European Affairs memo explained: "The Soviet Union will not resort to direct military action against the West in the near future and expects and counts on a period of several years of peace."[25]

Rather than a defence against possible Russian attack, NATO was largely conceived as a reaction to growing socialist sentiment in Western Europe. During WWII self-described communists opposed Mussolini in Italy, fought the fascists in Greece and resisted the Nazi occupation of France. As a result, they had a great deal of prestige after the war, unlike the wealth-holders and church officials who backed the fascists. If not for US/British interference, communists, without Moscow's support, would probably have taken power in Greece and won the 1948 election in Italy. In France the Communist Party won 30 percent of the first post-war vote, filling a number of ministries in a coalition government.

At the time of Italy's first post-war election Pearson's assistant, Escott Reid, explained that "the whole game of the Russians is obviously to conquer without armed attack."[26] For his part, Pearson decried an "attempt at a complete Russian conquest of Italy by constitutional or extra-constitutional means" and described class struggle by workers as a "new and sinister kind of danger, indirect aggression."[27]

Pearson demonstrated a great deal of interest in the ties between workers struggles and communist parties in Western Europe. Just after NATO's creation Pearson told the House: "In both France and Italy the large communist parties have suffered very serious setbacks in recent months in political prestige. Among the workers the use of the strike as primarily a political weapon for the furtherance of soviet aims was demonstrated in the attempt to bring down the French government in Paris. The strikes failed as did similar strikes attempting to upset the government of Italy ... Finland, Norway and Greece."[28]

US officials were equally concerned. George Kennan, the top US government policy planner at the time of NATO's formation, considered "the communist danger in its most threatening form as an internal problem that is of western society."[29] For his part NATO commander Dwight D Eisenhower explained: "One of the great and immediate uses of the [NATO] military forces we are developing is to convey a feeling of confidence to exposed populations, a confidence which will make them sturdier, politically, in their opposition to Communist inroads."[30]

Pearson expressed similar sentiments. In March 1949 he told the House: "The power of the communists, wherever that power flourishes, depends upon their ability to suppress and destroy the free institutions that stand against them. They pick them off one by one: the political parties, the trade unions, the churches, the schools, the universities, the trade associations, even the sporting clubs and the kindergartens. The North Atlantic Treaty Organization is meant to be a declaration to the world that this kind of conquest from within will not in the future take place amongst us."[31]

NATO planners feared a weakening of self-confidence among Western Europe's elite and the widely held belief that communism was the wave of the future. Minister Pearson explained in a 1948 memo to the Prime Minister: "Russia's allies in western Europe now are not so much the Communists as the forces of despair, apathy, doubt and fear. It therefore seems to me very important that the peoples of western democracies should make what [British Prime Minister] Mr. Attlee has called a bold move to raise in the hearts and minds and spirits of all those in the world who love freedom that confidence and faith which will restore their vigour."[32]

NATO strengthened the Western European elite's confidence to face growing left-wing parties and movements. Apparently, "Secret anti-Communist NATO protocols" committed alliance countries' intelligence agencies to preventing communist parties from gaining power.[33] After the fall of the Berlin Wall, information surfaced regarding groups the CIA and M-16 organized to "stay-behind" in case of a Soviet invasion of Western Europe. No invasion took place, of course. Instead, *NATO's Secret Armies* notes: "The real and present danger in the eyes of the secret war strategists in Washington and London were the at-times numerically strong Communist parties in the democracies of Western Europe. Hence the network in the total absence of a Soviet invasion took up arms in numerous countries and fought a secret war against the political forces of the left. The secret armies… were involved in a whole series of terrorist operations and human rights violations that they wrongly blamed on the Communists in order to discredit the left at the polls."[34]

Informally known as "Operation Gladio", these right-wing "stay behind" groups were overseen by NATO's Office of Security. A Spanish paper reported, in November 1990, "The Supreme Headquarters Allied Powers, Europe (SHAPE), directing organ of NATO's military apparatus, coordinated the actions of Gladio, according to the revelations of Gladio Secretary General Manfred Wörner during a reunion with the NATO ambassadors of the 16 allied nations."[35] As a result of the report the European Parliament condemned Operation Gladio and requested an investigation, which has yet to be undertaken.

Canada was one of two NATO countries omitted from Daniele Ganser's *NATO's Secret Armies* (Iceland was the other). No researcher has tied the two together, but the year after NATO was established the RCMP began a highly secretive espionage operation and internment plan known as PROFUNC (PROminent FUNCtionaries of the Communist Party). In October 2010 CBC's *Fifth Estate* and Radio-Canada's *Enquête* aired shows on "this secret contingency plan, called PROFUNC, [which] allowed police to round up and indefinitely detain Canadians believed to be Communist sympathizers."[36] In case of a "national security" threat up to 16,000 suspected communists and 50,000 sympathizers were to be apprehended and interned in one of eight camps across the country. Initiated by RCMP Commissioner Stuart Taylor Wood in 1950, the plan continued until 1983.

The plan was highly detailed. Police stations across the country would receive a signal to open their PROFUNC lists and apprehend said individuals. The "communists" would then be taken to "reception centres" where they would be restricted from talking and anyone attempting to flee would be shot. Eventually, the "communists" would be moved to one of the regional internment camps where their contact with the outside world would be limited to a single one-page letter each week. Their children would be sent to live with other family members.

Thousands of officers collected information used by PROFUNC at one time or another. Each potential internee had an arrest document (C-215 form) regularly updated with the person's physical description, age, photos, vehicle information, housing and sometimes the location of doors they might use to escape arrest.

Only a small number of the names on the list are public, but it clearly didn't take much to be put on it. *Enquête* uncovered the name of a 13-year-old girl who was on the list because she attended an anti-nuclear protest in 1964. Many prominent individuals were also on the PROFUNC list, including former Manitoba cabinet minister, Roland Penner, CBC President Robert Rabinovitch and NDP leader Tommy Douglas (who was voted greatest Canadian in a CBC poll).

Pearson had an incredibly expansive definition of NATO's defensive character. For him the north Atlantic pact justified European/North American dominance across the globe. As part of the Parliamentary debate over NATO Pearson said: "There is no better way of ensuring the security of the Pacific Ocean at this particular moment than by working out, between the great democratic powers, a security arrangement the effects of which will be felt all over the world, including the Pacific area."[37] Two years later he said: "The defence of the Middle East is vital to the successful defence of Europe and north Atlantic area."[38] In February 1953 Pearson went even further: "There is now only a relatively small [5000 kilometre] geographical gap between southeast Asia and the area covered by the North Atlantic treaty, which goes to the eastern boundaries of Turkey."[39]

In one sense the popular portrayal of NATO as a defensive arrangement was apt. After Europe's second Great War the colonial powers were economically weak while anti-colonial movements could increasingly garner outside support. The Soviets and Mao's China, for instance, aided the Vietnamese. Similarly, Egypt supported Algerian nationalists and Angola benefited from highly altruistic Cuban backing. The international balance of forces had swung away from the colonial powers.

To maintain their colonies European powers increasingly depended on North American diplomatic and financial assistance.

NATO passed numerous resolutions supporting European colonial authority. In the fall of 1951 Pearson responded to moves in Iran and Egypt to weaken British influence by telling Parliament: "The Middle East is strategically far too important to the defence of the North Atlantic area to allow it to become a power vacuum or to pass into unfriendly hands."[40] The next year Ottawa recognized the colonies of Vietnam, Cambodia and Laos as "associated states" of France, according to an internal report, "to assist a NATO colleague, sorely tried by foreign and domestic problems."[41] More significantly, during Pearson's time as foreign minister Canada gave France tens of millions of dollars in military equipment through NATO's Mutual Aid Program. These weapons were mostly used to suppress the Vietnamese and Algerian independence movements. In 1953 he told the House: "The assistance we have given to France as a member of the NATO association may have helped her recently in the discharge of some of her obligations in Indo-China."[42] Similarly, Canadian and US aid was used by the Dutch to maintain their dominance over Indonesia and West Papa New Guinea, by the Belgians in the Congo, Rwanda and Burundi and by the British in numerous places. Three years into the Alliance's creation Pearson boasted that his government had already distributed $324 million in mutual aid to NATO countries.[43]

NATO certainly strengthened European colonial authority. It was also designed to strengthen US influence around the world. Canada's External Affairs Minister saw the 1950-53 US-led Korean War as NATO's first test. In a history of the war David Bercuson writes: "Pearson seemed to be one of the very few who agreed with [President] Truman, [Secretary of State] Dean Acheson, and other American leaders that the Korean conflict was NATO's first true test, even if it was taking place half a world away."[44]

The role NATO played in North American/European subjugation of the Third World made Asians and Africans wary of the organization. To assuage these fears, in 1955 Pearson told a New Delhi audience that NATO would be dissolved when the "emergency" passed.[45]

Designed to maintain internal unity among the leading capitalist powers, NATO was the military alliance of the post-WWII US-centered multilateral order, which included the International Monetary Fund (IMF), World Bank, International Trade Organization (ITO) and the United Nations. (For its first two decades the UN was little more than an arm of the State Department. During the Korean War, for instance, Pearson "implied that the UN acted as the foreign-policy instrument of the Western alliance.")[46] Ottawa played a significant role in establishing all these institutions.

Canada was well placed to benefit from US-centered multilateral imperialism. A growing capitalist power, Canada was the world's second biggest creditor nation at the end of WWII (and had one of the biggest armies).[47] Additionally, the Canadian political and economic elite's close relations (through business, cultural or familial ties) with their US counterparts meant their position and profits were likely to expand alongside Washington's global position. For his part, Pearson argued that Canada would benefit from the growth in US power. During the Korean War, for instance, he said it was important to send a brigade because "Canada had every interest in strengthening the US position as leader in the struggle against Communism."[48]

In his outstanding 2011 book *Orienting Canada*, John Price describes the thinking at External Affairs after WWII. "What I am proposing is not just that the Canadian government played a supporting role in the emerging global order in which US power would predominate, a position that others have argued before, but, rather, that it actively encouraged the United States to take on this role, and that it did so due to the values shared by the men in the foreign-policy establishment of both countries — values that reflected ideas about race and empire, reinforcing their belief that the Euro-American powers had to play a significant role in Asia as well as elsewhere. In an era of decolonization, the Canadian government aligned the country with American imperialism."[49]

Pearson's role in the international negotiations over Palestine in 1947 is a prime example of "aligning the country with American imperialism." Under growing Zionist military pressure after World War II, Britain prepared to hand its mandate over Palestine to the newly created UN. In response, the US-dominated international body formed the First Committee on Palestine, which was charged with developing the terms of reference for a committee that would find a solution for the British mandate. Canada's Undersecretary of External Affairs, who made his sympathy for Zionism clear in a March 1945 speech, chaired the First Committee that established the United Nations Special Committee on Palestine (UNSCOP) in May 1947.[50]

At the First Committee Pearson rejected Arab calls for an immediate end to the British mandate and the establishment of an independent democratic country.[51] He also backed Washington's push to admit a Jewish Agency representative to First Committee discussions (ultimately both a Jewish Agency and Palestinian representative were admitted).

Pearson tried to define UNSCOP largely to facilitate Zionist aspirations. The Arab Higher Committee wanted the issue of European Jewish refugees excluded from UNSCOP but the Canadian diplomat worked to give the body a mandate "to investigate all questions and issues relevant to the problem of Palestine."[52]

A US State Department memo noted that Pearson "proved to be an outstanding chairman for [the First] Committee."[53] The Canadian Arab Friendship League, on the other hand, complained that the First Committee plan for UNSCOP was "practically irresponsible and an invitation to ... acts of terror on the part of Zionism." The League continued, Arabs would "never refrain from demanding for ... Palestine the same freedom presently enjoyed by other Arab states", newly independent from colonial rule.[54] Opposed to the idea that representatives from Canada, Guatemala, Yugoslavia and other countries should decide their future, Palestinians boycotted UNSCOP.[55]

Despite the objection of Prime Minister Mackenzie King, Undersecretary Pearson committed Canada to sending a delegate on the UNSCOP mission to Palestine.[56] In justifying his position to External Affairs Minister Louis St. Laurent, Pearson claimed "to have withdrawn our candidate at this moment might have been misinterpreted and have had an adverse effect on the discussion."[57] In fact, Pearson was significantly more willing to follow Washington's lead than the Prime Minister.

Canada's lead representative on UNSCOP, Ivan C. Rand, pushed for the largest possible Zionist state and is considered the lead author of the majority report in support of partitioning Palestine into ethnically segregated states. At the end of their mission the UNSCOP majority and minority reports were sent to the special UN Ad Hoc Committee on the Palestinian Question.

Not happy with Pearson's role in the First Committee, the Prime Minister would not allow the future Nobel laureate to chair the Ad Hoc Committee on the Palestinian Question despite Washington's request. Mackenzie King wrote that Pearson "lent himself perhaps too wholly to the desires of others," a coded reference to the State Department.[58] Still, he played a major role in the Ad Hoc Committee. At this forum Pearson rejected the Arab countries push to have the International Court of Justice decide whether the UN was allowed to partition Palestine. (Under US pressure, the Ad Hoc Committee voted 21 to 20 — with 16 abstentions — against allowing the International Court to adjudicate the matter).[59]

The Ad Hoc Committee was split into two subcommittees with one focusing on the partition plan and the other on a bi-national state. At the Ad Hoc Committee's Special Committee 1, Pearson worked feverishly to broker a partition agreement acceptable to Washington and Moscow. Preoccupied with the great powers, the indigenous inhabitants' concerns did not trouble the ambitious undersecretary. He dismissed solutions that didn't involve partition, which effectively meant supporting a Jewish state on Palestinian land. Responding to a bi-national plan proposed by the Ad Hoc Committee's Special Committee 2, he claimed: "The unitary state proposal meant nothing — a recommendation 'out of the blue and into the blue.'"[60] Pearson said: "a [Jewish] 'national home' was a sine qua non [essential condition] of any settlement."[61] He later explained: "I have never waivered in my view that a solution to the problem was impossible without the recognition of a Jewish state in Palestine. To me this was always the core of the matter."[62]

Pearson played a central role in Special Committee 1's partition plan. Both the *New York Times* and *Manchester Guardian* ran articles about his role in the final stage of negotiations.[63] Dubbed the "Canadian plan" the final Special Committee 1 agreement between the US and USSR on how to implement partition was "a result of the tireless efforts of Lester B. Pearson," according to a front-page *New York Times* article.[64] Some Zionist groups called him "Lord Balfour" of Canada and "rabbi Pearson".[65] In 1960 Pearson received Israel's Medallion of Valour and after stepping down as prime minister in 1968, he received the Theodore Herzl award from the Zionist Organization of America for his "commitment to Jewish freedom and Israel."[66]

By supporting partition he opposed the indigenous population's moral and political claims to sovereignty over their territory. Down from 90% at the start of the British mandate, by the end of 1947 Arabs still made up two-thirds of Palestine's population.[67] Despite making up only a third of the population, under the UN partition plan Jews received most of the territory. Pearson pushed a plan that gave the Zionist state 55% of Palestine despite the Jewish population owning less than seven percent of the land.[68] According to Israeli historian Illan Pappe, "within the borders of their UN proposed state, they [Jews] owned only eleven percent of the land, and were the minority in every district. In the Negev [desert]...they constituted one percent of the total population."[69]

Undersecretary Pearson was not supported by the Prime Minister, who wanted to align Canada more closely with London's position. While King was concerned about Britain, other government officials sympathized with the Palestinians. Justice Minister J.L. Isley said he was "gravely concerned" the push for partition did not meet the Arabs "very strong moral and political claims".[70] The only Middle East expert at External Affairs, Elizabeth MacCallum, claimed Ottawa supported partition "because we didn't give two hoots for democracy."[71] MacCallum's opinion wasn't popular with Pearson who organized late-night meetings allegedly to make it difficult for her to participate.[72] Despite failing to convince her boss at External Affairs MacCallum displayed sharp foresight. At the time of the partition vote, notes *The Rise and Fall of a Middle Power*, "MacCallum scribbled a note and passed it to Mike saying the Middle East was now in for 'forty years' of war, due to the lack of consultation with the Arab countries."[73] She was prescient, even if she did underestimate the duration of the conflict.

Far from being an "honest broker", a representative from the Canadian Arab Friendship League explained: "Our Canadian government at one time also favoured the creation of a federated State of Palestine which had at least some resemblance to a democratic solution. ... Mr. Lester B. Pearson and Mr. Justice Ivan C. Rand changed that official position of our government. Instead of the democratic solution, these gentlemen did their utmost to impose upon the Arabs the infamous partition scheme. The Arab world, I am sure, will remember them."[74]

A huge boost to the Zionist movements' desire for an ethnically-based state, the UN partition of British Mandate Palestine contributed to the displacement of at least 700,000 Palestinians. Scholar Walid Khalidi complained that UN (partition) Resolution 181 was "a hasty act of granting half of Palestine to an ideological movement that declared openly already in the 1930s its wish to de-Arabise Palestine."[75] About half the "ethnically cleansed" Palestinians were forced from their homes between November 1947 and May 1948, before any Arab army entered Palestine.[76] A number of massacres that left hundreds of Palestinian civilians dead prompted the Arab countries to enter the conflict. Israeli historian Benny Morris explains: "The events [massacres] of April 1948 — Deir Yassin, Tiberias, Haifa, Jaffa — rattled and focused their [Arab governments] minds, and the arrival of tens of thousands of refugees drove home the urgency of direct intervention."[77] In May 1948 Egypt and a number of other Arab countries declared war against the newly formed Israeli state. In response, notes *Canada and Palestine*, "Pearson would have liked to see passage of a US proposal to the Security Council to declare Egypt guilty of aggression and apply sanctions against her."[78] For his part, Mackenzie King wanted Canada to stick closer to the more ambivalent British position.

Not satisfied with taking the property of the Palestinian population living within the UN-defined Jewish state, during the 1948 war Israel grabbed 24% more land than it was allotted by the UN's (already unjust) Resolution 181. On November 4, 1948 the British, Chinese and Americans supported a resolution to force Israel to withdraw from territory it captured beyond the UN partition plan and to impose sanctions if it refused. Minister "Pearson was surprised", notes *Canada and the Birth of Israel*, "he had believed the U.S. would not back anything that included the threat of sanctions, and tried to convince the council to postpone action until Friday Five November, so that he could find out what the Americans were up to. The British and Americans would have none of this, however, and lobbied strongly for passage. Pearson resented their haste and tried not to be 'indecently rushed' but there was little he could do. At the evening session the resolution was adopted. Pearson voted for, but he strongly resisted a Lebanese and British effort to have it apply to Galilee as well the Negev."[79]

Pearson dismissed Arab claims that Israel enlarged her territory illegally — beyond the UN partition plan. He told the General Assembly "we must deal with the fact that a Jewish state has come into existence and has established its control over territory from which it will not be dislodged and we must address ourselves to the problem of regulating the relations of this community with its neighbors. I do not deny for a moment that this is a difficult circumstance for the Arab states to accept, but it is nevertheless the case."[80]

Despite working on the partition plan, after the 1948 war Pearson changed tack. His proposals left Israel in control of all its territorial gains, with no mention of the Palestinian state as proposed by the partition plan.[81] Similarly, when Israel proclaimed Jerusalem its capital in December 1949 Canada failed to advocate internationalization, which was called for in the 1947 partition plan. In December 1949 the General Assembly voted 38 to 14 in support of an Australian resolution calling for Jerusalem to be put under international control. With Pearson as External Affairs Minister Canada voted no.[82]

Troubled by Pearson's high profile support for Zionism, the Prime Minister blocked immediate Canadian recognition of Israel. After King retired in August 1948, the newly appointed External Affairs Minister moved to recognize a country that still lacked defined borders.[83] In a message to Israel's foreign minister, Pearson wrote "I have the honor to inform you, on behalf of the Government of Canada, that Canada recognizes de facto the state of Israel in Palestine, and that it also recognizes de facto the authority of the provisional Government of Israel, of which you are a member. This recognition is accorded in the knowledge that the boundaries of the new state have not as yet been precisely defined, and in the hope that it may be possible to settle these and all other outstanding questions in the spirit of the resolution adopted by the General assembly on December 11, 1948."[84]

What spurred Pearson's support for Israel? Jewish lobbying played no more than a tertiary part. The son of a Methodist minister, Pearson's Zionism was partly rooted in Christian teachings. His memoirs refer to Israel as "the land of my Sunday School lessons" where he learned that "the Jews belonged in Palestine."[85] One book on Pearson notes "there was a lot said at Sunday school about the historic home of the Jews but nothing about the Arab inhabitants."[86] At one point Canada's eminent statesman said he knew more about the geography of the holy land than of Ontario and in a 1955 speech Pearson called Israel (alongside Greece and Rome) the source of Western values.[87]

More practically, Israel's creation lessened the pressure on a widely anti-Semitic Ottawa to accept post-World War II Jewish refugees. At the end of the war the United Nations Relief and Rehabilitation Administration (UNRRA) was supposed to help resettle a couple hundred thousand displaced European Jews. When he was ambassador in Washington Pearson represented Canada at a number of UNRRA meetings where he faithfully defended the government's position against Jewish immigration.[88] After a meeting to discuss European refugees was moved from Ottawa to Bermuda, *None is Too Many* notes, "[Ambassador] Pearson exultingly wired [Undersecretary Norman] Robertson that the pressure was off and that, 'in the circumstances,' Ottawa was no longer 'a possibility' [to host the meeting]. And, he added, of even greater importance, Canada would not even be asked to take part in the conference."[89] Pearson believed sending Jewish refugees to Palestine was the only sensible solution to their plight.[90]

But the refugee issue was less of a concern than US-British relations. In 1947 Pearson was concerned with Anglo-American disunity over Palestine, more than the Palestinian crisis itself. "I wasn't thinking of trouble in terms of a war in Palestine," he explained. "I was thinking of trouble in terms of a grave difference of opinion between London and Washington. That always gives a Canadian nightmares, of course."[91] Pearson worried that disagreement between Washington and London over Palestine could adversely affect the US-British alliance and the emerging north Atlantic alliance.

Above all else, the ambitious diplomat wanted to align himself and Canada with Washington, the world's emerging hegemon. "Pearson usually coordinated his moves with the Americans," one book on Canada's role in the partition negotiations explained.[92] To determine their position on the UN Ad Hoc Committee, for instance, Canada's delegation "found it especially important to know the American's position."[93] A member of the Canadian delegation explained: "[we] will have nothing to say until after the United States has spoken."[94] Of central importance to Canadian support for partition was the belief that a Middle Eastern Jewish state would serve Western interests. An internal report circulated at External Affairs during the UN negotiations explained: "The plan of partition gives to the western powers the opportunity to establish an independent, progressive Jewish state in the Eastern Mediterranean with close economic and cultural ties with the West generally and in particular with the United States."[95]

In a 1952 memo to cabinet Pearson repeated this thinking. "With the whole Arab world in a state of internal unrest [after the overthrow of the British-backed monarchy in Egypt] and in the grip of mounting anti-western hysteria, Israel is beginning to emerge as the only stable element in the whole Middle East area."[96] He went on to explain how "Israel may assume an important role in Western defence as the southern pivot of current plans for the defence" of the eastern Mediterranean.[97] Pearson supported Israel as a possible western ally in the heart of the (oil-producing) Middle East. Two decades later he referred to that country as "an outpost, if you will, of the West in the Middle East."[98] Politically, culturally and economically dependent on North America and Europe, Israel was seen as a dependable Western imperial outpost.

On the Cold War, NATO and the creation of Israel, Pearson was clearly more concerned about siding with the emerging US empire than in following the principles enunciated in the UN Charter. This pattern continued throughout his career.

3. Minister for Fighting Asian Nationalism

World War II disrupted the balance of power in East Asia. During the war Japan occupied Dutch-controlled Indonesia and French Indochina (Vietnam, Cambodia and Laos). At the end of the war the Japanese were displaced from these countries as well as Korea and China. Washington and Moscow took charge of Korea while the Dutch and French tried to reassert control over their former colonies. At the same time a civil war raged in China.

Pearson generally sympathized with the European powers bid to regain their East Asian territories. He more forthrightly backed the growing US hegemon's attempts to subordinate the region to its designs. Pearson considered East Asia part of the "American sphere of influence."[1]

After World War II Mao's Communists fought Chiang Kai-shek's Kuomintang in the Chinese Civil War. Between 1945 and 1948 Ottawa provided the Kuomintang with 170 planes and $60 million in export credits while the US gave Chiang Kai-shek's forces hundreds of millions of dollars worth of military and non-military aid.[2] As the Communists were on the verge of taking control of the entire mainland, in 1949 Ottawa sent a naval vessel to

China. According to *Canadian Gunboat Diplomacy*, the boat was sent too late to stop the Kuomintang's defeat and was not needed to evacuate Canadians since British boats could do that. It seems that Pearson and Prime Minister St. Laurent wanted to demonstrate to the US and UK "that Canada was a willing partner", particularly in light of the emerging north Atlantic alliance.[3]

Mao's government was met with hostility from Ottawa. A November 1949 External Affairs memo stated "China must now be regarded as a potential enemy state." Steven Hugh further summarized the 1949 External Affairs report: "The rise of communist power on the mainland 'confronted the Atlantic Pact [NATO] powers with considerable strategic and political problems.' In Japan, argued the memo, the US position was threatened by a potentially hostile power in China; the usefulness of Korea and Taiwan as military bases would be undermined, and in Southeast Asia, 'the source of vital raw materials,' Western interests were menaced by the impetus the Chinese revolution gave to communist movements."[4]

That same month Pearson told Parliament: "A small revolutionary party there, espousing an alien philosophy, looking to the Soviet Union as the author and interpreter of that philosophy and as a guide in international relations, has seized military and governmental power throughout the greater part of China."[5] Seven years later the minister complained about China's "ruthless communist regime" and in another speech before the House he said the "strong, centralized, despotic and communistic regime on the mainland of China ... has ambitions to control and exploit the Asian peoples."[6]

Ottawa refused to recognize the Communist government. In June 1951 Pearson announced a trade embargo against China, telling Parliament "the Chiang Kai-shek government [based in Taiwan]...is the government of China we still recognize."[7]

Despite being portrayed as Soviet inspired, Mao's victory represented a major defeat for foreign powers by indigenous Chinese forces. Beginning in the 1820s the British began to dominate China. In two wars fought over trade and diplomatic relations, Chomsky notes, "the British government compelled China to open its doors to opium from British India, sanctimoniously pleading the virtues of free trade as they forcefully imposed large-scale drug addiction on China."[8] The Opium War of 1836 is considered by many to be the beginning of China's "Century of Humiliation".

Over the century Britain, France, Japan, Russia, Germany and the US all developed spheres of influence in China. The foreigners played the country's regions off against each other, keeping China's central government weak. Prior to Britain's arrival, a consolidated China dominated East Asia. As the oldest and most populous nation, a united China threatened Washington's plan to dominate the region. *Washington's China* describes the rabid hostility towards Mao's government among US decision-makers who complained of a Chinese centric worldview "as strong in Beijing today as it was under the Emperors centuries ago."[9] In short, American mandarins feared Chinese nationalism and worried that revolutionary nationalist ideology would spread throughout the region. Some within Canada's External Affairs department had similar concerns. They worried that "Communist China might dominate 'all Asian communist states' and form 'a new Asian alliance — linked neither with the Soviet Union nor the United States.'"[10]

After the Communists took control of China the US tried to encircle the country. They supported Chiang Kai-shek in Taiwan, built military bases in Japan and backed a right-wing dictator in Thailand. One of Washington's early objectives in Vietnam was to "establish a pro-Western state on China's southern periphery."[11] The success of China's nationalist revolution also spurred the 1950-53 Korean War in which eight Canadian warships and 27,000 Canadian troops participated. The war left as many as four million dead.

At the end of World War II the Soviets occupied the northern part of Korea, which borders Russia. US troops controlled the southern part of the country. A year into the occupation, a cable from Canadian diplomats in Washington, Ralph Collins and Herbert Norman, reported on the private perceptions of US officials: "[There is] no evidence of the three Russian trained Korean divisions which have been reported on various occasions ... there seems to be a fair amount of popular support for the Russian authorities in northern Korea, and the Russian accusations against the conservative character of the United States occupation in civilian Korea had a certain amount of justification, although the situation was improving somewhat. There had been a fair amount of repression by the Military Government of left-wing groups, and liberal social legislation had been definitely resisted."[12] Noam Chomsky provides a more dramatic description of the situation: "When US forces entered Korea in 1945, they dispersed the local popular government, consisting primarily of antifascists who resisted the Japanese, and inaugurated a brutal repression, using Japanese fascist police and Koreans who had collaborated with them during the Japanese occupation. About 100,000 people were murdered in South Korea prior to what we call the Korean War, including 30-40,000 killed during the suppression of a peasant revolt in one small region, Cheju Island."[13]

In sharp contrast to its position on Japan and Germany, Washington wanted the (Western dominated) UN to take responsibility for Korea in 1947. The Soviets objected, claiming the international organization had no jurisdiction over post-WWII settlement issues (as the US had argued for Germany and Japan). Instead, Moscow proposed that all foreign forces withdraw from Korea by January 1948.[14] Washington demurred, convincing member states to create the United Nations Temporary Commission on Korea (UNTCOK) to organize elections in the part of Korea occupied by the US. For its part, the Soviet bloc boycotted UNTCOK.

Undersecretary Pearson played an important part in having Canada join UNTCOK, which became contentious within cabinet. When the Prime Minister was out of the country External Affairs pushed cabinet to join UNTCOK but on his return to Ottawa, Mackenzie King objected. Privately, King described UNTCOK as "an effort on the part of the United States to put us into sharing the responsibility vis-à-vis Russia in the action taken or against the acceptance of the Russian suggestion."[15] For the Prime Minister, Washington turned to the UN to implement policies it was unable to pursue on its own.[16] King argued "the State Department was simply using the United Nations as an arm of that office to further its own policies."[17]

Worried about the long-term ramifications of UNTCOK and unhappy about the active role Canadian diplomats played in the UN's Palestine negotiations, King sent Undersecretary Pearson to Washington to try and extricate Canada from the Korea Commission. Pearson later called this his hardest assignment ever, making it clear in his biography that he tried to help the State Department.[18] *Diplomacy of Fear* described his role this way:

"Pearson acted as an intermediary to Washington: or more precisely, as the State Department's adviser on how to deal with Canada's eccentric prime minister. Finally a letter from President Truman to the prime minister, drafted with Pearson's advice, flattered King and emphasized the need for Canadian statesmanship."[19]

During the power struggle over Canada's participation in UNTCOK, External Affairs Minister Louis St. Laurent threatened to resign. Pearson agreed with St. Laurent's move. "I said [to St. Laurent] that I felt I should either resign or ask for an appointment abroad: that I really could not carry on in the department when policies with which I did not agree with were being laid down by the Prime Minister."[20] For his part, King wrote in his diary: "Pearson had been thrown into the situation under pressure from the United States and had yielded in order to help them out."[21] The prime minister believed the external affairs undersecretary was much "too ready to be influenced by American opinion."[22] In another entry King explained, "I really think [former undersecretary Norman] Robertson's judgment is sounder than Pearson's on these international affairs, and that he would be better at the head of the department here."[23]

St. Laurent and Pearson ultimately forced the outgoing prime minister to accept Canadian participation in UNTCOK, but King was proven right. The UN sponsored election in South Korea led to the long-term division of that country and Canada's involvement in a conflict that would cause untold suffering. On May 10, 1948 the southern part of Korea held UNTCOK-sponsored elections. In the lead-up to the election leftwing parties were harassed in a campaign to "remove Communism" from the south. As a result leftwing parties refused to participate in elections "wrought with problems" that "provoked an uprising on the island of Cheju, off Korea's southern coast, which was brutally repressed."[24]

After the poll Canada was among the first countries to recognize the Republic of Korea in the south, effectively legitimizing the division of the country.[25] Pearson sent Syngman Rhee, who became president, a note declaring "full recognition by the Government of Canada of the Republic of Korea as an independent sovereign State with jurisdiction over that part of the Korean peninsula in which free elections were held on May 10 1948, under the observation of the United Nations Temporary Commission."[26] Conversely, Ottawa refused to recognize the North, which held elections after the South, and opposed its participation in UNTCOK reports. For Pearson the South held "free elections" while those in the North "had not been held in a democratic manner" since the Soviets did not allow UNTCOK to supervise them.[27] After leaving office Pearson contradicted this position, admitting "Rhee's government was just as dictatorial as the one in the North, just as totalitarian. Indeed, it was more so in some ways."[28]

The official story is that the Korean War began when the Soviet-backed North invaded the South on June 25, 1950. The US then came to the South's aid. As is the case with most official US history the story is incomplete, if not downright false. *Korea: Division, Reunification, and US foreign Policy* notes: "The best explanation of what happened on June 25 is that Syngman Rhee deliberately initiated the fighting and then successfully blamed the North. The North, eagerly waiting for provocation, took advantage of the southern attack and, without incitement by the Soviet Union, launched its own strike with the objective of capturing Seoul. Then a massive U.S. intervention followed."[29]

Korea was Canada's first foray into UN peacekeeping/peacemaking and it was done at Washington's behest. US troops intervened in Korea and then Washington moved to have the UN support their action, not the other way around. On June 28 Pearson lied to Parliament, telling the House that Washington acted on behalf of the international organization because the troops foreseen in the UN charter did not exist.[30] "In this case the United States recognized a special responsibility which it discharged with admirable dispatch and decisiveness."[31] In reality American troops landed 24 hours before the UN endorsed military action and President Truman told the press they would intervene 11 hours before the UN voted to support the mission.[32]

The UN resolution in support of military action in Korea referred to "a unified command under the United States."[33] Incredibly, United Nations forces were under US General Douglas MacArthur's control yet he was not subject to the UN.[34] Canadian Defence Minister Brooke Claxton later admitted "the American command sometimes found it difficult to consider the Commonwealth division and other units coming from other nations as other than American forces."[35]

After US forces invaded, Ottawa immediately sent three gunboats. Once it became clear US forces would not be immediately victorious, Pearson began lobbying to mount "some kind of international force" for Korea.[36] In his *Memoirs* he explained "I was anxious that Canada should assume a full responsibility by sending an expeditionary force. There were, however, members of the Cabinet ... who did not support a forward foreign policy."[37] Both the Prime Minister and Defence Minister were wary about committing Canadian ground troops with Claxton fearing the US was "getting [Canada] into something to which there is really no end."[38] But, Pearson pressed his colleagues hard.[39] In an August 3, 1950 letter to Prime Minister St. Laurent, Pearson insinuated that he'd quit as external affairs minister if Canada failed to deploy ground troops to Korea.[40]

Canada's famed peacekeeper pushed to send troops into an extremely violent conflict. Two million North Korean civilians, 500,000 North Korean soldiers, one million Chinese soldiers, one million South Korean civilians, ten thousand South Korean soldiers and 95,000 UN soldiers (516 Canadians) died in the war.[41] The fighting on the ground was ferocious as was the UN air campaign. US General MacArthur instructed his bombers "to destroy every means of communication and every installation, factory, city and village" in North Korea except for hydroelectric plants and the city of Rashin, which bordered China and the Soviet Union, respectively.[42]

A *New York Times* reporter, George Barrett, described the scene in a North Korean village after it was captured by UN forces in February 1951:

"A napalm raid hit the village three or four days ago when the Chinese were holding up the advance, and nowhere in the village have they buried the dead because there is nobody left to do so. This correspondent came across one old women, the only one who seemed to be left alive, dazedly hanging up some clothes in a blackened courtyard filled with the bodies of four members of her family.

"The inhabitants throughout the village and in the fields were caught and killed and kept the exact postures they had held when the napalm struck — a man about to get on his bicycle, fifty boys and girls playing in an orphanage, a housewife strangely unmarked, holding in her hand a page torn from a Sears-

Roebuck catalogue crayoned at Mail Order No. 3,811,294 for a $2.98 'bewitching bed jacket — coral.' There must be almost two hundred dead in the tiny hamlet."[43]

The above story captured Pearson's attention. In a letter to the Canadian ambassador in Washington, Hume Wrong, he wondered how it might affect public opinion and complained about it passing US media censors. "[Nothing could more clearly indicate] the dangerous possibilities of United States and United Nations action in Korea on Asian opinion than a military episode of this kind, and the way it was reported. Such military action was possibly 'inevitable' but surely we do not have to give publicity to such things all over the world. Wouldn't you think the censorship which is now in force could stop this kind of reporting?"[44]

Cold War Canada summarizes the incredible violence unleashed by UN forces in Korea: "The monstrous effects on Korean civilians of the methods of warfare adopted by the United Nations — the blanket fire bombing of North Korean cities, the destruction of dams and the resulting devastation of the food supply and an unremitting aerial bombardment more intensive than anything experienced during the Second World War. At one point the Americans gave up bombing targets in the North when their intelligence reported that there were no more buildings over one story high left standing in the entire country ... the overall death toll was staggering: possibly as many as four million people. About three million were civilians (one out of every ten Koreans). Even to a world that had just begun to recover from the vast devastation of the Second World War, Korea was a man-made hell with a place among the most violent excesses of the 20th century."[45]

After the outbreak of a series of diseases at the start of 1952 China and North Korea accused the US of using biological weapons. Though the claims have neither been conclusively substantiated or disproven — some internal documents are still restricted — in *Orienting Canada* John Price details Pearson's highly disingenuous and authoritarian response to the accusations, which were echoed by some Canadian peace groups. While publically highlighting a report that exonerated the US, Pearson concealed a more informed External Affairs analysis suggesting biological weapons could have been used. Additionally, when the *Ottawa Citizen* revealed that British, Canadian and US military scientists had recently met in Ottawa to discuss biological warfare, Pearson wrote the paper's owner to complain. Invoking national security, External Affairs "had it [the story] killed in the *Ottawa Journal* and over the CP [Canadian Press] wires." Price summarizes: "Even without full documentation, it is clear that the Canadian government was deeply involved in developing offensive weapons of mass destruction, including biological warfare, and that Parliament was misled by Lester Pearson at the time the accusations of biological warfare in Korea were first raised. We know also that the US military was stepping up preparations for deployment and use of biological weapons in late 1951 and that Canadian officials were well aware of this and actively supported it. To avoid revealing the nature of the biological warfare program and Canadian collaboration, which would have lent credence to the charges leveled by the Chinese and Korean governments, the Canadian government attempted to discredit the peace movement."

Pearson cheered on the fighting in Korea. On May 14, 1951 he told Parliament that the only viable solution to the Korean conflict was "to continue inflicting heavy losses on the aggressors" and called on the UN to "do so much damage to the forces of communist aggression that before long they will see reason. It may then be possible to negotiate with them on United Nations terms."[46] Directed against China, this statement ignored Beijing's repeated attempts — rebuffed by Washington — to end the fighting. In a controversial move, two years into the conflict Washington decided to bomb hydroelectric power stations on the Yalu River that provided much of northern China's electricity. While some British and Canadian politicians protested this escalation of tactics Pearson felt the operation was "within existing military directives" and was ordered "with military considerations solely in mind."[47]

Canadian troops denigrated the "yellow horde" of North Korean and Chinese "chinks" they fought.[48] One Canadian colonel wrote about the importance of defensive positions to "kill at will the hordes that rush the positions."[49] A pro-military book notes dryly that "some [soldiers] allowed their Western prejudices to develop into open contempt for the Korean people."[50]

Crimes committed by Canadian troops, even against allied South Koreans, largely went unpunished. Those found guilty of murdering or raping Korean civilians were usually released from prison within a year or two after legal experts and civilian judges in Ottawa reviewed their cases. In one disturbing example, a half dozen Canadian troops who beat South Korean soldiers and then raped and killed two South Korean women barely spent any time in jail.[51] "The Canadian military justice system," Chris Madsen explained, "showed astounding lenience towards these men's criminal actions."[52] In light of Canadians attitudes and actions it's not surprising that Koreans were hostile towards Canada's presence. Lieutenant Chris Snyder said Koreans "so plainly didn't want us to be there."[53] In fact, two months into the US invasion a press report, read into the House, explained "the U.S. Soldier in Korea is a lonely man fighting in a land of sullen strangers. The peasant does not seem to care when the invaders [North Koreans] are on his doorstep. Often, he must be forcibly evacuated from the land which is about to become a battlefield. He gives no sign that he regards the Americans as anything but intruders disturbing the peace of his slow-moving life."[54]

A series of factors led to the war. For starters, North Korean leader Kim Il-sung wanted to reunite the country under his authority, which didn't bother Moscow or Beijing. In *The Hidden History of the Korean War* famed journalist I.F. Stone argues that the US and two of its main regional allies also wanted war. In an election three weeks before the fighting Syngman Rhee lost control of South Korea's Parliament, which wanted to reunify the country. A war Rhee could blame on the North would weaken those calling for peaceful reunification of the country, thereby strengthening his hand. For his part, Chiang Kai-shek, the leader of Formosa (Taiwan), worried that more countries would follow Britain and recognize China's Communist government, undermining his ability to speak on behalf of China at the UN Security Council and elsewhere. Chiang believed the regional tension created by war would deter other countries from recognizing Mao's government, which is what happened with Canada.

Washington, particularly the general in charge of the US occupation of Japan, backed Rhee and Chiang's position. More generally, Korea gave Washington a pretext (outlined two months earlier in infamous National Security Council statement NSC 68) to strengthen its position in the region and to ramp up military spending.[55] Privately, Secretary of State Dean Acheson admitted as much. He said "Korea came along ... [and] created the stimulus which made [for] action" on NSC 68 and provided "an excellent opportunity ... to disrupt the Soviet peace offensive, which... is assuming serious proportions and having a certain effect on public opinion."[56] Acheson further admitted that the decision to fight in Korea was "a purely political one" that "had made it politically possible for the United States to secure congressional and public support for a quick and great increase in defense expenditures; for further assistance to those of its friends who are willing to make a similar increased effort; for the imposition of needed controls, higher taxes, the diversion of manpower in the armed forces and defense industries, etc."[57]

In many ways the Korean War marks the beginning of the permanent war economy in the US. The Korean War helped bring the US economy out of a slight recession and put to rest talk of a post-World War II depression (WWII ended the Great Depression).[58]

The Korean War served similar economic purposes in Canada. It justified a dramatic increase in military spending, or in the words of the head of the official opposition, George A. Drew, the "dreadful necessity of a vast rearmament program."[59] The day before Drew spoke, Pearson told Parliament that because of "the situation throughout the world and the crisis in Korea ... we must increase our own military preparations ... Measures which are dictated by considerations of national security and, indeed, of national existence."[60]

Though some might quibble over whether the Korean civil war threatened this country's existence, Canadian participation definitely strengthened this country's ties to the US economy.[61] A joint US-Canada industrial mobilization planning committee met two months into the war and, according to a history of Canada's role in Korea, decided "that study should be made of the basic industrial programs of the two countries and of the steps necessary to meet the production and supply requirements involved."[62] The Korean War also increased the ties between the Canadian and American militaries. For the first time Canadian troops relied on American support weapons.[63]

Pearson openly admitted that "the strategic consequences of the loss of Korea would not be serious," yet he still claimed, "the moral consequences would be grave in the extreme. A state which had been created by the United Nations would have been destroyed by naked aggression. And other countries, particularly in South and Southeast Asia, which are open to communist attacks would be disheartened and demoralized."[64] In other words, if the West's allies in South Korea lost the civil war then other countries might question their dependence on Washington. If that happened the dominoes might all come tumbling down.

Canada's intervention in Korea went beyond defending the South Korean regime. After pushing North Korean troops back to the 38th parallel, the artificial line that divided the North and South, the UN force moved to conquer the entire country. Pearson supported the UN resolution allowing foreign troops to cross the 38th parallel.[65] The US-led force continued north in a bid to undermine China's Communist government. American officials, particularly UN force commander Douglas MacArthur, repeatedly attacked China's Communist government. Before China entered the war American aircraft bombed that country while carrying out air missions in northern Korea.[66] Even more ominous, both MacArthur and (later) President Truman publically discussed striking China with nuclear weapons.

UN troops pushed north even after the Chinese made it clear that they would intervene to block a hostile force from approaching their border. Beijing was particularly worried about northern China's dependence on energy from the Yalu River power station in northern Korea.

Six months after the US intervened in the Korean civil war the UN voted to brand China an aggressor in the conflict.[67] Yet Beijing only sent forces into Korea after hundreds of thousands of hostile troops approached its border. From the Chinese perspective the People's Liberation Army defended the country's territorial integrity, which was compromised by US bombings and the control of Formosa by foreign backed forces. Secretary of Cabinet Norman Robertson and acting External Affairs Undersecretary Escott Reid lobbied Pearson to vote against the UN motion describing China as an aggressor. The minister responded: "Norman, you have no idea what the pressure is like down here [at the UN in New York]. I can't."[68] In his *Memoirs* Pearson explained: "We were faced with great American pressure to support the resolution of condemnation [of China]. We succumbed to that pressure."[69] But, Pearson also justified the UN resolution. "I said that we would support the US resolution because we could not deny the fact that Chinese forces were participating in aggression."[70] His other reason for voting to condemn China's role in Korea was Washington's benevolent foreign policy. "Our support for this resolution", Pearson declared, "was easier for us in view of the fact that it had been submitted by the United States, which was taking the leadership 'in the defense of freedom everywhere'."[71] (A few years later he made an even more absurd statement, claiming "it is inconceivable to Canadians, it is inconceivable certainly to me, that the United States would ever initiate an aggressive war."[72])

Washington used the UN's condemnation of China to justify excluding the world's most populous nation from the UN, a situation that lasted until 1971. It was also used to block China from participating in the post-WWII peace treaty between Japan and 48 countries. During the September 1951 Japanese peace conference Pearson echoed the US State Department's argument for excluding China from the UN-based agreement. He said: "The Beijing government must realize that ... it cannot shoot its way into the United Nations."[73]

India and Russia criticized the US-led Japan peace conference. India said it would not sign a treaty "which would in effect make Japan a United States bastion against [China]."[74] For their part, the Soviets criticized China's exclusion from the peace conference because they were the primary victims of Japanese aggression before and during WWII. The USSR also complained that the treaty ceded several Japanese islands to the US military and violated China's sovereignty over Taiwan and a number of other islands.

Minister Pearson ignored international criticism of the treaty and disregarded Undersecretary of External Affairs Arnold Heeney's advice. Heeney believed Canada should only haltingly support the peace treaty with Japan yet, according to *Contradictory Impulses*, Pearson "lined up solidly behind the United States."[75]

Pearson publically challenged India for criticizing the treaty and praised General MacArthur and President Truman's appointee on the matter, John Foster Dulles, for their work.[76] He said "it [the treaty] reflects also the wisdom and basic democracy of the United States government and people in refusing to embark on the imperialistic course of making Japan a mere appendage to the United States; or more subtly perhaps, of attempting to refashion Japan in the image of America."[77]

But, this is largely what Washington did. It took Japan more than six years to sign a post-WWII peace treaty even though the country was demilitarized and democratized by the fall of 1947.[78] At this point most countries, including Canada, were prepared for Japan to regain its sovereignty. At an August 1947 Commonwealth meeting in Australia the head of the Canadian delegation, Defence Minister Brooke Claxton, reflected the unanimous opinion when he declared a "peace conference [with Japan] should be called without delay."[79] But Washington wanted to extend its occupation to thwart leftwing forces in the country and to further integrate Japan into its East Asia network. Early on the US occupation was relatively progressive, but in February 1947 MacArthur banned a general strike and then in the summer of 1948 he sent foreign troops to break a strike at a movie studio and ended government employees' rights to collective bargaining.[80] An October 1947 US Policy Planning Staff study concluded that there were "great risks in an early relinquishment of Allied control over Japan. It [the US] has no satisfactory evidence that Japanese society would be politically or economically stable if turned loose and left to its own devices at this stage. If Japan is not politically and economically stable when the peace treaty is signed, it will be difficult to prevent communist penetration."[81] In large part, Washington maintained its occupation of the country to help Japan regain its economic strength as the US-backed regional leader. Noam Chomsky explains: "Japan was to be developed not only as a military base against China and the Soviet Union, but also as an industrial base supporting a counterrevolutionary cause in Southeast Asia."[82]

Supportive of the US occupation of Japan, Pearson saw no benefit in pressing Washington to organize a peace conference if American officials did not feel the time was right.[83] Canada's most decorated statesman backed Washington's policy despite objections from External Affairs colleagues. *Contradictory Impulses* notes "Pearson largely dismissed the concerns of Canada's top Japanese specialist, the controversial diplomat Herbert Norman, about Allied occupation policy."[84] In late 1948 undersecretary Pearson drafted the basis of Canada's position on the Allies occupation of Japan. He wrote: "The present United States policy of denying Japan's industrial potential to the Soviet Union is of great importance and should be supported. While we had hoped that it might have been possible to convene a Japanese Peace Conference at an early date we do not think we would be justified in pressing the United States government unduly to push forward with a conference at this time if they do not think this wise."[85]

After World War II the British tried to reassert control over Malaya with its large tin and rubber production. In response to an increasingly repressive colonial authority an anti-British insurgency began in 1948. It was rooted in the poor and disenfranchised Chinese minority (about one in six Malays).

Canada's external minister was hostile to the insurgency. Before the House he described the resistance as "communist terrorism" and "communist bandits, and it is right to call them that."[86] Pearson explicitly supported the colonial authority, referring to British "commitments" in Malaya.[87] In June 1952 he told Parliament "There has been some improvement since [British] General [Gerald] Templer took command, but it is still far from stable. The efforts that are being made to stamp out communist banditry are making progress but it is discouraging to realize that only four or five thousand of these bandits in the jungles of Malaya have been able to create this problem which has persisted for so many years."[88] In praising Templer Pearson failed to mention the General's policy of denying food to areas supporting the rebels, which included spraying herbicide on crops.[89] To weaken the rebels' support base, the British also forcibly relocated 500,000 Malays, a large portion of the population.[90]

During World War II Japan took Indonesia from the Dutch. To strengthen their hold on the country the Japanese destroyed the colonial state and encouraged latent anti-Dutch sentiment. Two days after Japan surrendered on August 15, 1945 nationalist leaders Sukarno and Hatta declared Indonesian independence. But the Dutch refused to accept the loss of this valuable colony and tried to reestablish control through force of arms. Between 45,000 and 100,000 Indonesians died in four years of fighting, while many more were wounded or displaced.[91]

Though he conceded that Dutch actions were highly unpopular in Asia, Pearson sympathized with their position.[92] Canada opposed a series of Security Council motions censuring the Netherlands. At one point during UN negotiations he wrote the Prime Minister "I do not see that there is much more that we can do for the Netherlands at this point… although we shall continue to consider their position most sympathetically, and shall do what we can to make the resolution [on steps towards independence] more acceptable to them."[93]

Ottawa sold the Netherlands weapons as they suppressed anti-colonial resistance, even though Canada's Commonwealth ally, Australia, banned arms sales to the Netherlands.[94] Canada's support for the Dutch upset Canberra. An Australian official called Canada "the mouthpiece of Holland", notes *Fire and the Full Moon*.[95] "Australian officials were aggrieved that Canada was providing what they saw as blanket support to the Netherlands instead of listening to the regional Commonwealth power. Things came to a head when [Australian High Commissioner F.M.] Forde handed a blistering aide-memoire to Pearson immediately after December's Security Council vote."[96]

The same book also notes: "The US government tried to find a position somewhere between the Netherlands and Indonesian nationalists; Ottawa was much less concerned about seeking Indonesian goodwill. Instead it settled on a 'middle course' between the Dutch and American positions, seeking to straddle the ground between Canadian allies."[97]

As was the case elsewhere, Pearson was mostly concerned with NATO, not the merits of Dutch control over Indonesia. His primary aim was "to prevent a conflict between the United States and the Netherlands that could harm progress toward the North Atlantic alliance."[98]

The Netherlands finally recognized Indonesian sovereignty in December 1949, but the Dutch maintained control over West Papua New Guinea. Just off its coast, Indonesia considered West Papua part of its landmass. Jakarta also worried that Dutch control of West Papua threatened their hard-fought independence. In 1954 Indonesia pushed the Dutch to relinquish West Papua. On a train to Boston Pearson decided that "Canada would be one of the few countries [at the UN] to switch from abstaining [on West Papua independence] to voting against, which reduced Indonesian support below the two thirds needed to pass."[99] External Affairs did not think highly of Papuans. "Civilization is still in a very primitive stage," explained a Canadian memo. It continued "[democracy for] the headhunters of New Guinea [was] out of the question."[100]

As with the Dutch, Pearson defended France's bid to maintain control of its former Asian colonies. The only difference was that his support was more forthright because Washington

Lester Pearson's Peacekeeping

fully backed the French, which was not the case with the Dutch in Indonesia.

During World War II, Japan invaded French Indochina. Throughout the war the French colonial administration — under the Nazi-backed Vichy regime — acted as a Japanese puppet. In 1941 the Ho Chi Minh led Viet Minh Front launched an independence struggle, liberating considerable portions of northern Vietnam. After the Japanese surrendered to the Allies in August 1945, the Viet Minh seized control of the northern city of Hanoi and proclaimed the Democratic Republic of Vietnam.

The West supported the Viet Minh's fight against the Japanese and Vichy Regime. But after WWII the US, Chiang Kai-shek's China and Britain backed France's bid to reassert control over Vietnam. In November 1946 the French killed 6,000 in the northern port city of Haiphong, initiating the French Vietnam War.[101] During eight years of fighting French forces tortured and killed tens of thousands of Vietnamese.

French atrocities didn't deter Pearson from publicly defending Paris and their preferred Vietnamese politicians. In February 1950 he wished France's puppet President Bao Dai "every success".[102] Pearson added that Paris "deserve[s] our gratitude" for "the progress towards freedom in that area which the French government are seriously sponsoring [in Vietnam]."[103] The next year Pearson told the House: "If the valiant efforts now being made by France to defend and complete the independence of Indochina were to fail, the whole of southeast Asia, including Burma, Malaya and Indonesia, with their important resources of rubber, rice and tin, might well come under communist control."[104]

Pearson called Vietnamese resistance to French colonialism "communist aggression". Implying the nationalist forces were directed from Moscow, he claimed that "Soviet colonial authority in Indochina" was stronger than French rule.[105] In 1954 the Canadian minister said "military action by the Viet Minh represented the real threat to Indochina" and upon the French defeat at Dien Bien Phu Pearson released a statement to that country's foreign minister (repeated by the Prime Minister in the House).[106] "With all free men, Canadians, while lamenting the tragic ending of the legendary conflict at Dien Bien Phu, salute with pride and honour the historic defenders of the fortress."[107]

Pearson backed up his words with diplomatic and material deeds. Canada endorsed NATO's conclusion that France's war in Indochina was in "the fullest harmony with the aims and ideals of the Atlantic community." Norway and Denmark dissented from the majority position.[108] At the end of 1952 Ottawa supported France's bid to accord "recognition to Vietnam, Cambodia and Laos as associated States of Indo-China within the French Union in accordance with the terms of agreements between France and the respective states."[109] This recognition made Colombo Plan aid available to "countries" Ottawa privately admitted "do not fulfill the customary legal requirements and which are frowned upon by most of the neighboring countries in Asia."[110]

Between 1950 and 1954 some $61.3 million worth of Canadian arms, bullets, aircraft and engines were used by the French in Indochina.[111] *Towards a Francophone Community* notes: "Pearson believed that France's war against communism in Indo-China deserved Canada's support, but Louis St. Laurent and Minister of Defence Brook Claxton worried about how the Canadian public would react to sending Canadian military supplies to help France retain its colonial position in South East Asia. ... The Canadian cabinet approved the transfer of the Canadian equipment without any such restrictions by agreeing to send Mutual Aid equipment to France itself. ... The French were told that what they did with the supplies after their arrival in France was of no concern to the Canadian government."[112]

Despite support from Ottawa and a billion dollars in aid from Washington, the French failed to suppress the anti-colonial struggle.[113] After the French defeat at Dien Bien Phu in the spring of 1954, both Secretary of State John Foster Dulles and President Dwight Eisenhower called Pearson and Prime Minister St. Laurent to ask what they thought about a full-scale US intervention in Vietnam, including a possible nuclear strike in support of the French.[114] The Canadian politicians failed to object though Pearson expressed some reservations about using nuclear weapons.

After losing Dien Bien Phu, the French agreed to a settlement. The Geneva Accords (not to be confused with the Geneva Convention) ended the First Indochina War with a Viet Minh controlled north and a Western-backed regime in charge of the south. According to the agreement, internationally sponsored elections to unify the country were to be held within 48 months. The International Control Commission (ICC) for Vietnam was set up with Canada representing the West, Poland the Eastern bloc and India supposed to be neutral. Alongside these two other countries Canada was mandated to enforce the implementation of the Geneva Accords and the peaceful reunification of Vietnam. But, notes *Orienting Canada*, "Pearson's initial instructions to him [Sherwood Lett, Canada's first ICC commissioner] indicated that the government perceived the Geneva Accords as a means by which to stop communism in Asia."[115]

Washington ignored the Geneva Accords and recognized South Vietnam, escalating its campaign against Vietnamese nationalism. Most countries viewed the South Vietnamese regime, which carried out many extrajudicial assassinations and held thousands of political prisoners, as little more than a French/American puppet. As such they refused to initiate relations, but on December 20, 1955, Canada recognized South Vietnam, effectively breaking the Geneva Accords.[116]

Knowing their candidate would lose, Washington blocked the planned elections to unify the country. Privately, President Eisenhower admitted that Ho Chi Minh, the leader of the north, would have won by a wide margin. He wrote in his memoirs: "I have never talked or corresponded with a person knowledgeable in Indochinese affairs who did not agree that had elections been held at the time of the fighting, possibly 80 percent of the population would have voted for the Communist Ho Chi Minh as their leader rather than Chief of State Bao Dai."[117]

On a couple occasions Pearson effectively called on Saigon to ignore the required election and break the Geneva Accords. Pearson described "the understandable reluctance on the part of the Diem government to take part in any elections unless they can be given absolute assurance that these will be free elections, in our meaning of the word. They have no confidence in the communist authorities in the north in bringing that about."[118] In another instance he said: "I am very much afraid that there will not be elections of a kind which we would consider free. I am even more afraid of the fact that we might be maneuvered into the wrong kind of elections. That might be the greater danger of the two. Still I think we can be pretty certain that the government of the southern part of Vietnam will not participate in any elections which would ensure the victory of communism, at least in the South, by making it impossible for anybody to vote non-Communist. That is not the kind of free elections that they have in mind."[119] A few weeks after Pearson made this statement External Affairs instructed its representative to the ICC "not to encourage in any way this commission taking part in" pre-election discussions.[120] South Vietnam used a Canadian ICC amendment to justify its refusal to hold elections, which ultimately led to millions dying in the Second Indochina War.[121]

Soon after the ICC was established, some of the 170 Canadian soldiers and officials sent to Vietnam started spying for the US. In November 1954 Pearson asked Ambassador Arnold Heeney to make sure information given to Washington by Canadian ICC commissioners "is for their background use only and under no circumstances should be disseminated publicly or referred to in public. Should it become generally known that we are passing any information to the United States government concerning the activities of the international commissions [ICC] it would have very serious repercussions for our representatives on the commissions and we would have to reconsider the whole policy of passing on information to the United States."[122]

During the early Cold War years Canada is said to have had a "special relationship" with India. Ottawa distributed a significant amount of aid to the world's second most populous nation in a bid to keep it within the Western fold. Or, as Pearson put it, "one of the jobs of a Canadian in New Delhi would be to help disabuse Indians of their more extreme prejudices against the United States."[123] Canadian influence over India was apparent at the ICC for Vietnam. India often sided with Canada in support of US military policy, despite India's history of colonial domination not unlike Vietnam's. Canadian, British and US aid to India, which dwarfed what Poland or the USSR offered, played no small role in India's stance.

From the get go geopolitical considerations were the primary motivation for disbursing foreign assistance in Asia. With Mao's triumph in China in 1949, Canada began its first significant (non-European) allocation of foreign aid through the Colombo Plan. The Colombo Plan's primary aim was to keep the former British Asian colonies, especially India, within the Western fold. Or as a 1957 internal department assessment explained: "It is to offer some hope, and to provide a sense of international co-operation, to the ruling and politically effective groups in Asian countries ... to reduce the attractiveness of Communism to these groups."[124]

To justify an initial $25 million ($250 million today) in Colombo Plan aid Pearson told the House: "Communist expansionism may now spill over into South East Asia as well as into the Middle East ... it seemed to all of us at the [Colombo] conference that if the tide of totalitarian expansionism should flow over this general area, not only will the new nations lose the national independence which they have secured so recently, but the forces of the Free World will have been driven off all but a relatively small bit of the great Eurasian landmass. In such circumstances it would not be easy to contemplate with equanimity the future of the rest of the world. ... We agreed at Colombo that the forces of totalitarian expansionism could not be stopped in South Asia and South East Asia by military force alone."[125]

If some of India's post-colonial population had not set their sights on a socialist/nationalist solution to their troubles — with the possibility of Soviet or Chinese assistance — Canada probably would not have provided aid. Five years into the Colombo Plan, Pearson admitted "Canada would not have started giving aid if not for the perceived communist threat."[126] In an August 1956 speech calling on Parliament to increase aid outlays he said: "If nothing else, it is a matter of self-defence. Apparently the Soviet Union is going all out in an attempt to gain the minds of the so-called underdeveloped countries."[127] During his speech to the House Pearson described the problem of "[Soviet] infiltration into the economies of other countries through economic assistance."[128] Social Credit MP John Blackmore asked the minister what he meant by "infiltration". Pearson replied: "It means that the supplying government, the assisting government, by virtue of its economic assistance, will achieve an influence which will be more than economic and the country which is getting the assistance will probably become more and more dependent on the supplying government; or it may mean that economic assistance is given with political strings attached which would provide for infiltration." This prompted Blackmore to ask if this "resembles what the United States [or Canada?] is doing when she gives an export subsidy"? The minister replied tersely, "I did not have the United States in mind when I just spoke."[129] Of course, it's only "infiltration" when an enemy does it. It's called "aid" when we do it.

4. A Commitment to Democracy?

Pearson claimed to support democracy against totalitarianism. In 1955 he waxed eloquent about "the struggle of free, expanding progressive democracy against tyrannical and reactionary communism."[1] Despite the rhetoric, Pearson backed the US Central Intelligence Agency's most infamous early coups.

In 1953 the US and Britain overthrew Iran's first popularly elected Prime Minister, Mohammad Mossadegh. After the coup the country was handed over to a brutal regime that ruled for 26 years. Pearson's External Affairs department played a small part in overthrowing Iranian democracy. In the lead-up to the coup the British embassy in Tehran represented Canada's diplomatic relations in the country and the files at External Affairs on Iran largely consist of US and British reports. Thirteen months before the coup Canada's ambassador in Washington cabled Ottawa: "The situation in Iran could hardly look worse than it does at present. Mossadegh has been returned to power with increased influence and prestige and will almost certainly prove even more unreasonable and intractable than in the past, so that a settlement of the oil dispute will be harder than ever to arrange."[2]

Mossadegh wanted Iran to benefit from its huge oil reserves. But the British had different plans. As one of the earliest sources of Middle Eastern oil, the Anglo-Iranian Oil Company (British Petroleum's predecessor) had generated immense wealth for British investors since 1915. Unwilling to yield any of its profits, Anglo-Iranian chairman Sir William Fraser responded to Iran's attempts to gain a greater share of its oil wealth by proclaiming "one penny more and the company goes broke."[3] Yet a 1952 State Department report showed the company was selling its oil at between ten and thirty times its production cost.[4] Needless to say, Anglo-Iranian Oil was unpopular. Even the US State Department noted the company's "arrogance had made it genuinely hated in Iran."[5] In the face of Anglo-Iranian intransigence, Mossadegh defied the English, supporting the nationalization of the country's oil industry. It was a historic move that made Iran the first former colony to reclaim its oil.

Canada's external affairs minister was not happy with the Iranians move. In May 1951 Pearson told Parliament the "problem can be settled" only if the Iranians keep in mind the "legitimate interests of other people who have ministered to the well-being of Iran in administering the oil industry of that country which they have been instrumental in developing."[6] Later that year Pearson complained about the Iranians' "emotional" response to the English. He added: "In their anxiety to gain full control of their affairs by the elimination of foreign influence, they are exposing themselves to the menace of communist penetration and absorption — absorption into the Soviet sphere."[7]

In response to the nationalization, the British organized an embargo of Iranian oil, which Ottawa followed.[8] The embargo weakened Mossadegh's government, enabling the CIA's subsequent drive to topple the nationalist prime minister. After a March 11, 1953 National Security Council Meeting, the head of the CIA, Allan Dulles, gave the agency's Tehran bureau a million US dollars ($8 million today) to be used, "in any way that would bring about the fall of Mossadegh."[9] *All the Shah's Men* explains: "Through a variety of means, covert agents would manipulate public opinion and turn as many Iranians as possible against Mossadegh. This effort, for which $150,000 was budgeted, would 'create, extend and enhance public hostility and distrust and fear of Mossadegh and his government'. It would portray Mossadegh as corrupt, pro-communist, hostile to Islam, and bent on destroying the morale and readiness of the armed forces. While Iranian agents spread these lies, thugs would be paid to launch staged attacks on religious leaders and make it appear that they were ordered by Mossadegh or his supporters."[10]

Pearson did not protest the overthrow of Iran's first elected prime minister. Privately, External Affairs celebrated. Three days after Mossadegh was ousted, a cable from the ambassador in Washington explained: "Perhaps the most disturbing and unpredictable factor [in Iran] was the continued strength of the Tudeh party."[11] Iran's Communist Party, Tudeh, pushed for the nationalization of the Anglo-Iranian Oil Company and its support for Mossadegh was used to justify the coup. Reflecting British-American demonization/criminalization efforts, External Affairs sent the RCMP a copy of a UK government report titled the "Tudeh Party of Persia".[12]

When some Canadians asked External Affairs "to prevent the imprisonment or execution of premier Mossadegh of Iran" they were told nothing could be done.[13] Four months after the coup, Canada's ambassador in Washington cabled Ottawa about "encouraging reports from their [US] embassy in Tehran on the growing strength of the present [coup] government."[14] Canada followed the lead of the UK and US in doing business with the brutal dictatorship of Mohammad-Reza Shah Pahlavi. Pearson's External Affairs began diplomatic relations with Iran in 1955.[15]

Emboldened by their success in Iran, in late 1953 the CIA launched Operation PBSUCCESS to overthrow Guatemalan President Jacobo Arbenz. They conducted an extensive propaganda campaign to undermine Arbenz, which included promoting a Guatemalan "liberation army" they built up in Honduras. Under the command of exiled army officer Colonel Carlos Castillo Armas this small military force coordinated their attacks on the country with the CIA. As part of these efforts the US Navy enforced a sea blockade of Guatemala while American warplanes buzzed Guatemala City to sow popular panic and dissent within the army. In the face of this onslaught, Guatemala's elected president stepped down and a series of military men took his place.

Arbenz ran afoul of Washington decision-makers when he gave landless peasants uncultivated land owned by the United Fruit Company (The Boston-based company was offered compensation at the price they valued the property for tax purposes). "By far the largest property owner in the country", 85% of United Fruit's 550,000 acres of land was unused in 1953.[16] The company monopolized Guatemala's banana exports, its telephone and telegraph facilities as well as its main Atlantic harbour and nearly every mile of railroad track in the country.[17] Thomas McCann, a 20-year United Fruit employee, summarized the company's history in Guatemala: "Guatemala was chosen as the site of the company's earliest development activities at the turn of the century because a good portion of the country contained prime banana land and because at the time we entered Central America, Guatemala's government was the region's weakest, most corrupt and most pliable. In short, the country offered an 'ideal investment climate,' and United Fruit's profits there flourished for fifty years. Then something went wrong: a man named Jacobo Arbenz became president."[18]

Beyond United Fruit, Washington worried that Arbenz's social democratic policies would disrupt the elite-dominated status quo in the region. In 1954, a State Department official was unusually blunt, pointing out that "Guatemala has become an increasing threat to the stability of Honduras and El Salvador. Its agrarian reform is a powerful propaganda weapon; its broad social program of aiding the workers and peasants in a victorious struggle against the upper classes and large foreign enterprises has a strong appeal to the populations of Central American neighbors where similar conditions prevail."[19] Arbenz represented the threat of a bad example.

Similar to Iran, the coup against Arbenz was a "definitive blow to Guatemala's young democracy." It led to a series of dictatorships and a three decade long civil war that cost more than 100,000 people their lives.[20]

Despite CCF questioning in the House, Pearson refused to acknowledge US involvement in the invasion of Guatemala. He said: "To the best of my knowledge, based on information we have received, the attacking forces in Guatemala seem to be Guatemalan, though some non-Guatemalans might be included."[21] The minister admitted that he had foreknowledge that "matters" in Guatemala "would be reaching a climax very shortly", but claimed not to know what would bring the situation to a head.[22]

Pearson also helped isolate Arbenz. In 1953 External Affairs refused the Guatemalan foreign minister's request to open embassies in each other's countries. A similar request was denied again the next year.[23] Prior to Arbenz's 1950 election, a study by Canada's trade commissioner in Guatemala claimed that "businessmen and landowners do not have any cause to view the prospect of Arbenz as future president with any optimism."[24]

Northern Shadows, an outstanding history of Canada's role in Central America, summarizes: "At External Affairs and in Canadian [corporate] boardrooms, the coup [against Arbenz] was chalked up as another victory of the Free World against the [Soviet] Menace."[25]

On top of these assaults against Iranian and Guatemalan democracy, minister Pearson accepted the exclusion of Africans from political life in their own countries. He pursued policies sympathetic to South Africa's apartheid regime, which emerged during his time as foreign minister. In 1948 the National Party took power and quickly passed laws classifying South Africans by race and "barring people from living, operating businesses or owning land anywhere else but in the areas designated for each race."[26] These laws strengthened the white minority's grip over most of the country's land and created a large pool of easily exploitable black labourers. South Africans who protested were met with repression. Under the Suppression of Communism Act newspapers were banned and some 8,500 dissidents were jailed through December 1952.[27]

During Pearson's time as minister Canada opposed or abstained on numerous UN resolutions challenging South African racism.[28] In December 1949 he told Parliament: "We have had close and very friendly cooperation with the South African delegation at the [UN] assembly."[29] For Pearson, the apartheid system was a domestic matter and thus beyond the scope of the UN. He didn't believe the General Assembly "competent to interfere in the domestic affairs of member states by certain types of resolutions or by setting up committees and commissions to visit those countries and report and possibly take action at succeeding assemblies."[30] After one General Assembly vote South Africa's permanent representative at the UN reported the "behind the scenes lobbying of Canadian and American delegates in support of South Africa had been 'especially valuable.'"[31]

In 1952 South Africa's high commissioner in Ottawa called Pearson and Canada's Ambassador to the UN, Paul Martin Sr., "good friends of South Africa" with whom he "got on famously".[32] The praise reflected their record. Canada's position at the UN helped the apartheid regime and during this period South African officials regularly visited First Nations reserves to draw insights into controlling their Black population.[33]

When Pearson was foreign minister the vast majority of Africans were excluded from shaping their own destiny. The British, Belgians, Portuguese and French dominated the continent and there is little evidence to suggest that he did anything to change this state of affairs. Throughout his time as minister, for instance, Canada's relations with British Africa were overseen by London yet there seems to be no indication of Pearson opposing our complicity in African colonialism. Instead Pearson lauded the United Kingdom's "big contribution" to "the defence of freedom generally" and in January 1957 he told the House: "No people in the world have proved themselves more 'dependable defenders of freedom' than have the British."[34] In that speech he added: "Those countries which still have direct responsibilities for non-self-governing territories [colonies] should not be made to feel at the United Nations or elsewhere that they are oppressors to be deprived arbitrarily of their rights or indeed their reputations."[35]

While Canada's famed diplomat effectively backed British colonialism in Africa local populations did not. The Ghanaians who fought with the Allies during WWII spearheaded the independence struggle in the late 1940s. Groups in Nigeria, Tanzania, Uganda and elsewhere increasingly demanded freedom from British rule. The Kikuyu in Kenya (the largest ethnic group) launched an anti-colonial struggle in 1952 and over the next eight years 50,000 Kenyans were killed in what became known as the "Mau Mau Uprising". The British were responsible for horrific massacres in a near genocidal campaign against the Kikuyu. Pearson was aware of developments in Kenya and the rest of British Africa but he said little.[36]

In North Africa the French delayed granting Tunisia and Morocco independence. To avoid antagonizing Paris Pearson backed the French position. "In autumn 1952 ... the Canadian delegation voted against all the resolutions introduced by African and Asian states that urged France to recognize the independence of Tunisia and Morocco and sought to create a committee of good offices to assist in negotiations between France and the north African nationalists. Instead, the delegates expressed Canada's faith in France's intentions towards Tunisia and Morocco and stressed that it should be allowed to fulfill them without interference from the United Nations."[37]

Pearson waited until June 1956 to offer formal Canadian recognition and the External Affairs Minister opposed the Department of Citizenship and Immigration's bid to facilitate French immigration from Morocco and Tunisia, which could have lessened anti-colonial tension.[38] Pearson opposed French immigration, notes *Towards a Francophone Community*, because he "believed that Canada's overriding interest in the area was to maintain its friendship for the West and its close ties with France."[39] More significantly, Pearson sided with France against Algeria's independence movement. In November 1954 the Front de Libération Nationale officially began its struggle against the colonial authority. The French ruled Algeria since 1830 and 1,400,000 million French settlers lived there, many of whom had been there for generations. To suppress the resistance, French forces killed hundreds of thousands while displacing many more. Prominent historian Pierre Vidal-Naquet believes the French military were responsible for "possibly hundreds of thousands of instances of torture" in Algeria.[40]

Pearson supported the French diplomatically, for example conceding when Paris demanded that Algeria be included in NATO even though it was a colony and outside the North Atlantic region.[41] In a March 1949 House of Commons speech on NATO he implied that Algeria was part of France. A minute after describing Article 6 of the organization as including the "Algerian departments of France", Pearson said NATO "does not include colonial possessions."[42] In 1955, when African and Asian states tried to have the Algerian conflict debated at the UN, Canada opposed the move.[43] *Towards a Francophone Community* explains: "Increasingly concerned for France's political stability, in January 1957 [External Affairs Undersecretary] Jules Leger again tried to persuade Lester Pearson that the time had come to get the French government to accept the eventual independence of Algeria as the basis for a negotiated end to the war. Pearson was not convinced, arguing that no country could exert enough pressure to change France's Algerian policy and that any attempt to do so would run afoul of the strength of French national feeling ... Pearson did not want to jeopardize France's enthusiasm for NATO by an ill-advised attempt at peace brokering in Algeria."[44] During his time as foreign minister the Canadian government gave France tens of millions of dollars in military equipment under NATO's Mutual Aid Program, which was supposed to deter Soviet aggression in Western Europe.[45] "Even with 400,000 troops in Algeria, in autumn 1956, Canada continued to provide the French military with extensive gifts of armament."[46] Pearson obviously knew that Paris was using Canadian weapons in Algeria. To formalize the obvious, in March 1956 the federal government modified the Defence Appropriation Act, which required Canadian Mutual Aid supplies be used to defend western Europe.[47]

While Ottawa backed the French, North Africa's most populous nation, Egypt, supported the Algerian struggle after it gained full independence. Formally independent since 1922, the country became truly sovereign when Gamal Nasser's Free Officers Movement overthrew the British backed monarchy in 1952. In response Pearson made a number of statements in the House about the importance of the Middle East to the West and the risk of communist penetration. In one instance he said "[Canada] regrets exceedingly the action taken by the Egyptian government to repudiate the [quasi-colonial] Anglo-Egyptian treaty of 1936."[48] Nasser's rise to power sparked Canada's interest in Egypt and pushed this country's leadership closer to Israel. In 1954 Ottawa opened an embassy in Cairo "because of the importance to the free world of maintaining peace in this strategic area," according to an External Affairs report.[49] The next year Pearson visited Egypt "to warn Nasser against the historic Russian designs in the Mediterranean and the Middle East."[50]

Canadian arms sales to Israel grew alongside concern about Egypt's political orientation. A 150-page thesis documenting

Canadian weapons sales to Israel between 1948 and 1956 explains: "Pearson openly told Israeli ambassador Michael Comay that its arms applications would be considered more favorably because of Nasser's apparent unreliability."[51]

Canada continued selling Israel weapons after the UN censored it for killing dozens of Egyptians and Palestinians in the Egyptian-controlled Gaza Strip in 1954 and 1955.[52] In 1956 Israeli pilots came to train in Canada and Ottawa agreed to sell that country 24 top-of-the-line F86 fighter jets.[53]

These weapon sales did not go unnoticed in Egypt. In September 1956 Nasser condemned Ottawa for selling Israel weapons. "The supplying of Israel with arms despite her repeated aggressions against Arab frontiers is considered a hostile act aimed at the whole Arab nation."[54]

Ottawa agreed to sell Israel weapons at a particularly politically tumultuous time. In July 1956 Nasser nationalized the Suez Canal Company, which British and French interests controlled. Outraged at this challenge to their authority in the region, the former colonial powers plotted to overthrow Nasser. Three months after Egypt nationalized the assets of the Suez Canal Company, British, French and Israeli officials decided to coordinate an attack against Egypt. According to the plan, Israel would invade up to the Sinai Peninsula and then London and Paris would call for Israeli and Egyptian troops to withdraw from the Suez Canal area, splitting Egypt in two. The two former Middle East powers would then argue that Egypt's control of this important shipping route was insecure and needed to be placed under British-French management.

On October 29, 1956 Israel airdropped a battalion into the Sinai. Fighting ensued and the next day the English and French called on Egypt and Israel to vacate the area around the Suez

Canal. Unsurprisingly, Egypt refused so the French and English launched air attacks on Egyptian targets, allegedly to separate the belligerents.

Both Moscow and Washington immediately condemned the invasion of Egypt. Sixty-four countries voted for a US resolution to the UN criticizing the Israeli invasion. Five countries opposed this initial vote and Pearson made Canada one of six countries to abstain.[55]

At the time of the Suez Crisis Washington still wanted to work with Nasser and the growing anti-monarchist movement in the region. US decision-makers feared that British/French actions would push parts of the Arab world closer to the Soviets unless they opposed their European allies actions forcefully. Additionally, Washington criticized the French/British invasion to send a message to the former colonial powers that the US was the new master in this geostrategically important region. Beyond publically denouncing Paris and London's actions, Washington demonstrated its displeasure by selling British currency and blocking London from acquiring much needed IMF funding.[56] For their part, the Russians threatened to send troops to defend Egypt and to strike London and Paris with nuclear missiles.[57]

Pearson won the 1957 Nobel Peace Prize for his role in establishing the peacekeeping force that helped resolve the Suez Crisis. Ever since, peacekeeping has been a major part of the Canadian identity. Memorialized on a postage stamp and the ten-dollar bill, Parliament passed a motion in 2007 for a peacekeeping day.

During the Suez Crisis Pearson undermined the former European colonial powers position. As a result Linda McQuaig claims "Pearson's distaste for colonialism played a role in what ended up being a significant diplomatic and foreign policy triumph: his handling of the 1956 Suez Crisis."[58] There's little evidence to suggest he was motivated by any "distaste for colonialism". In fact, Pearson's main concern was disagreement between the US and UK over the intervention, not Egyptian sovereignty or the plight of that country's people. The minister explained that Canada's "interest is prejudiced when there is division within the Commonwealth or between London, Washington or Paris."[59] Maintaining the seven-year-old NATO alliance was Pearson's priority when he intervened in Egypt in the fall of 1956.

After coordinating with US Secretary of State John Foster Dulles, Pearson proposed sending an international force to Egypt to remove the invading armies. Dulles said the US "would be happy if Pearson formulated" a plan to keep the peace and Washington offered to transport troops from their home countries to join the UN mission in Egypt.[60]

Although he clearly sided with the Americans, Canada's foreign minister also sought to help extricate Britain and France from their disastrous plan. Upon learning about British actions St. Laurent wanted to send London a scathing diplomatic note but Pearson convinced the angry Prime Minister to soften his tone.[61] On October 31 he told Dulles "we are interested in helping Britain and France. I would like to make it possible for them to withdraw with as little loss of face as possible and bring them back into realignment with the U.S."[62]

Pearson initially suggested that the UN simply declare the British and French soldiers en route to Egypt to be peacekeepers (London and Paris claimed their goal was to separate warring Israeli and Egyptian forces). There was little interest in this idea so he then proposed that other countries dispatch troops to

Egypt under UN control. But Pearson didn't believe his proposal would pass if British and French forces en route landed before the General Assembly agreed to create a UN force to separate the belligerents. He needed Britain's cooperation for the plan to work. "It's vitally important that they [Britain and France] slow down now to give us a chance," Pearson told Norman Robertson, Canada's High Commissioner in London. Robertson convinced the British to delay their troops from landing on condition the UN vote on Canada's proposal the following evening.[63]

Pearson made numerous declarations sympathetic to the aggressors. He said UK/French/Israeli actions took place "against the background of those repeated violations and provocations."[64] Early in the UN negotiations Canada's foreign minister said he would try to postpone or amend any resolution critical of Britain or France.[65] A month after the invasion Pearson declared "I do not for one minute criticize the motives of the governments of the United Kingdom and France ... I may have thought their intervention was not wise, but I do not criticize their purposes."[66]

The primary "purpose" of the invasion was to re-establish European control over the Suez Canal and to weaken Arab nationalism. France wanted to put an end to Nasser's support for Algeria's independence movement while Israel's main objective was to destroy Egypt's military before it became a credible deterrent. As we've seen, the famed statesman sympathized with the French position in Algeria and sold weapons to Israel to counter Egypt. He also repeated Britain's claim that nationalizing the Suez Canal, which included full financial compensation, would somehow destabilize the region. (Privately, the British cabinet recognized that Nasser's nationalization "amounted to no more than a decision to buy out shareholders."[67])

Before the invasion Pearson declared Canada's "support for the principle of international control of the Suez canal."[68] He complained: "The violation by the government of Egypt of an international convention governing the use of an international waterway so important as the Suez Canal is, of course, to be condemned. Possibly it should be recalled at this time that the convention in question attempted to safeguard the free use of the waterway in war and peace. In that sense, the convention was already violated by the Egyptian government when the Israeli vessels were prevented from using the canal."[69]

After the canal was nationalized, Ottawa haltingly supported Britain's move to freeze Egyptian assets in Canada. *Pearson's Peacekeepers* notes: "The Canadian government advised the Canadian Banker's Association that financial institutions may wish to keep in mind the questionable legality of Egypt's actions [nationalization of the canal] if any requests were received to release assets held in Canada."[70]

Pearson also (obliquely) threatened Egypt. Prior to the invasion, he said "it is devoutly to be hoped that President Nasser will accept this invitation to negotiate a peaceful and permanent solution of this serious problem ... a failure to do so would involve a very heavy responsibility indeed."[71]

Some have concluded that during the Suez Crisis Pearson wanted "a compromise that would, in part, 'legitimize' the Franco-British action."[72] This thesis is supported by the fact that British forces initially provided the UN troops with motor transport and Canada took over protecting English interests in the country.[73] Additionally, British Prime Minister Anthony Eden called for "police action [in Egypt] ... to separate the belligerents and to prevent the resumption of hostilities between them. If the U.N.

were then willing to take over the physical task of maintaining peace, no one would be better pleased than we."[74] After the conclusion of hostilities the leaders of all three invading countries spoke in support of Canadian actions in Egypt.[75] In his memoirs Eden claimed the United Nations Emergency Force (UNEF) was his idea and the British Prime Minister thanked Pearson. "Never have I seen action on the part of a government that excited me more than the rapid way you [Pearson] and your government moved into the breach with your proposal for a United Nations force to go to Suez. You did a magnificent job, and we admire it."[76]

Pearson's pronouncements regarding the UK/France/Israel intervention initially led Cairo to reject Canadian troops. Ottawa's membership in NATO also made Egypt suspicious of Canada's motivations.[77] Cairo was correct to worry about Canadian participation in the military mission. This is how one Canadian peacekeeper explained his posting to Egypt: "I thought we [were] here to clear the Egyptians out of the canal zone. Instead damned if they aren't treating us like prisoners of war."[78]

Contrary to the views of Arab countries, India and many other former colonies, Pearson saw the UN troops largely as an occupation force. During the first meeting of the UNEF advisory committee he raised the issue of who controlled the UN troops.[79] After another 200 Canadian troops were deployed to the Middle East in March 1957 Pearson told the House: "No consultation with the government of Egypt by the Secretary-General or any agent of the Secretary-General was required or took place, as there was no question of Egypt's consent being necessary."[80]

At a time when Egypt was militarily weak, he used the UN force's presence to demand policy changes, warning Nasser in the spring of 1957 that UN troops would leave if he continued to pursue nationalistic reforms. Pearson elaborated: "We feel that Egypt had the right to be consulted and to agree to the entry of an international force, but having given that consent as she did, she has no right to control the force, to order it about, to tell the force when it shall leave. If Egypt is dissatisfied with the operation of the force, or if anybody else is dissatisfied, or if Egypt wants the force to withdraw, feels its work is completed, Egypt should make its views known to the Secretary-General who would take it up with the Committee of Seven [of which Pearson was a member] and then it would go to the full assembly, and until the assembly had decided the force would carry on."[81]

Israel's view of the international force was similar. Israel believed UNEF "cannot be subordinated to Egypt's desires. Its movements and its composition cannot be the subject of dictation by the host country."[82] Pearson proposed placing UNEF on Egyptian soil. He never made a serious push to station any UN troops on the territory of the (local) aggressor. "Israel would not accept foreign troops upon her soil," explained Prime Minister David Ben-Gurion.[83]

The Suez crisis created a rift between Canada and Israel, but it was short-lived. Pearson later summarized Canada's position vis à vis Israel: "We worked as hard as we possibly could with the Americans to get their support for a resolution which would lay down in detail specifically the arrangements we should follow for the withdrawal of foreign troops and Israeli troops from Egypt. We weren't successful. We did our best to modify their attitude. We also told them, and in no uncertain terms, that if they supported a resolution of sanctions against Israel, we would have to break with them because we would not support it in those circumstances."[84]

Lester Pearson's Peacekeeping

Pearson did press Israel to remove its troops from Egypt but he did so with the country's interests in mind. After France and England pulled out, he told Israeli officials to withdraw or "you run the risk of losing all your friends."[85]

Pearson's bias against Egypt was also on display regarding the Gaza Strip. He wanted to remove Gaza from Egyptian administration and make it a UN controlled area. Canada's foreign minister called on the UN to "accept responsibility to the maximum possible extent for establishing and maintaining effective civil administration in the Gaza Strip."[86] This proposal was rejected by the Arab countries as it would have made it more difficult to expose Israeli aggression towards Palestine. Syria's spokesperson at the UN said "the representative of Canada is trying to show various faces in various directions. Canada is deftly supporting the Zionist policy."[87] For his part, Jordan's representative reminded the General Assembly that Pearson played an important role in the partition plan that created a Jewish state on Palestinian land.[88]

Pearson helped keep the peace in Egypt, but it was between two sides of a dispute within NATO. Canada's policies and actions assisted declining powers Great Britain and France save face over a disastrous invasion and those actions were supported by the new superpower, the United States. This is hardly a shining example of an "honest broker" or peacekeeper.

5. Riding the Atom Bomb to the Prime Minister's Office

Despite his reputation as a peacekeeper Pearson played an important role in Canada's nuclear journey. For starters, he promoted uranium extraction in his Algoma East riding near Sudbury, Ontario.[1] More significantly, the Nobel peace laureate and the rest of the Liberal cabinet allowed the US to station nuclear weapons on Canadian soil. The first "nuclear weapons came to Canada as early as September 1950, when the USAF [Air Force] temporarily stationed eleven 'Fat Man'- style atomic bombs at Goose Bay Newfoundland."[2] Beginning in 1952 Ottawa gave the US Strategic Air Command the okay to train in Canadian air space with nuclear-armed aircraft.[3] At the same time, the US Atomic Energy Commission carried out military tests north of the border to circumvent oversight by American "watchdog committees." As part of the agreement with Washington, Ottawa committed to prevent any investigation into the military aspects of nuclear research in Canada.[4]

On the diplomatic front, Pearson also supported his ally's nuclear weapons. Just after he became external minister, in August

1948, Ottawa voted against a UN call to ban nuclear weapons and in December 1954 Pearson voted to allow NATO forces to accept tactical nuclear weapons through the alliance's policy called MC 48, The Most Effective Pattern of NATO Military Strength for the Next Few Years.[5] According to *Canada and UN Peacekeeping*, Pearson "was integral to the process by which MC 48 was accepted by NATO."[6]

During his time as foreign minister Canada always voted with the US on nuclear policy in disarmament talks.[7] *Pearson and Canada's Role in Nuclear Disarmament and Arms Control Negotiations 1945-1957* explains: "Pearson consistently supported the increase in Western nuclear might" and he "believed that the United States needed all the military hardware it could acquire."[8] In early 1956 External Affairs ruled out banning nuclear tests in this country because they "improve[ed] our nuclear defense potential."[9]

Any disagreement Pearson had with Washington's nuclear policy at a five-country (USSR, US, France, Britain and Canada) disarmament commission set up in 1954 was kept quiet.[10] Author Joseph Levitt reports: "So great was his desire to ensure American nuclear supremacy over the Soviet Union that he agreed to policies" he ostensibly opposed.[11] Levitt also details how Pearson used nuclear disarmament negotiations to score anti-Soviet propaganda points.[12] No matter the responsibility, he blamed failed negotiations on the Soviets. Privately, Pearson referred to "the propaganda advantages which we might expect to gain either if the negotiations were resumed or by demonstrating publicly that it is the Russians and not we who are dragging our feet on this issue."[13] On another occasion he tried to place "upon the Russians the burden of refusing [an agreement]."[14]

On an issue of domestic interest Pearson repeatedly lied. The book *Canadian Nuclear Weapons* describes one instance where he was "guilty of significantly stretching the truth."[15] On another occasion he said Canada had not "acquired" nuclear weapons, even though more than 150 Royal Canadian Air Force aircraft in Europe carried them.[16] In 1954 Pearson lied to Parliament, claiming "although Canada was a partner in the wartime project to develop atomic weapons, nevertheless as soon as the war was over the Canadian project was directed entirely toward nonmilitary objectives."[17]

Pearson dismissed civil society groups demanding nuclear disarmament. When the Canadian Peace Congress called for the atomic bomb to be outlawed, he said "a victim is just as dead whether he is killed by a bayonet or atom bomb."[18] Later, he bitterly denounced the Peace Congress. *Cold War Canada* explains: "Pearson's campaign against the Peace Congress took him to such small and unimportant places as a young persons' current events club in Toronto, where he delivered a dire warning that the peace issue was a 'Communist-inspired campaign,' and the Peace Congress 'the trap so cunningly baited by the Communists and their sympathizers.' They should not be regarded as idealists searching for peace, but 'as the instruments, even indeed the completely willing and skillful instruments, of a ruthless conspiracy which is intent on destroying the free world and imposing its powerful system of abominable repression everywhere.' After quoting the Stockholm Appeal, which called for the total ban on all nuclear weapons and branded any nation making first use of nuclear weapons 'criminal,' Pearson tore the mask off this seemingly innocuous statement. 'It is surely significant that this Communist-sponsored petition seeks to eliminate the only decisive weapon possessed by the West at a time when the Soviet Union and its friends and satellites possess a great superiority in all other types of military power.'"[19]

The Nobel laureate called for individuals to destroy the Peace Congress from the inside. Pearson publically applauded 50 engineering students who swamped a membership meeting of the University of Toronto Peace Congress branch. He proclaimed: "If more Canadians were to show something of this high spirited crusading zeal, we would very soon hear little of the Canadian Peace Congress and its works. We would simply take it over."[20]

Nuclear politics even played a part in Pearson's 1963 move from Stornoway, house of the opposition leader, to the PM's residence at 24 Sussex Drive. Pearson criticized Prime Minister John Diefenbaker for not adequately supporting Washington during the October 1962 Cuban Missile Crisis. After a number of attempts by Washington to either overthrow the Cuban government or assassinate Fidel Castro, Havana sought nuclear missiles. Unhappy about American nuclear weapons in Turkey capable of striking Moscow, the Soviets were prepared to oblige the Cubans. Washington freaked out when they discovered the Soviets and Cubans were building bases for nuclear missiles in Cuba with the ability to hit major US centres. The Americans organized a sea blockade of the island nation and in the subsequent game of chicken between Moscow and Washington the world came to the brink of nuclear war. Fortunately, Soviet naval officer Vasili Arkhipov blocked the needed three officer consensus and opposed launching a nuclear tipped torpedo from a submarine trapped by 11 US war ships.

During the Cuban Missile Crisis the Kennedy administration wanted Ottawa's immediate and unconditional support in putting the North American Aerospace Defense Command (NORAD) on high alert. Diefenbaker hesitated, unsure if Washington was telling him the full story about Soviet/Cuban plans or once again bullying the small island nation. For his part, notes *Kennedy and Diefenbaker*, "Pearson publicly and solidly endorsed Kennedy's actions [during the Cuban missile crisis]."[21] The leader of the opposition claimed that Diefenbaker put the US under unnecessary threat and he questioned the Prime Minister about Canadian-owned ships trading with Cuba.[22] On October 9, *The 1962 Cuban Missile Crisis* notes, "Pearson picked up the gauntlet by asking Diefenbaker if he was going to do anything about the latest US concern over Canadian owned ships in the Cuban trade."[23] One reporter asked Diefenbaker at the time: "Mr. Pearson, the leader of the opposition in the House of Commons, in a statement tonight, endorsed President Kennedy's action, including the quarantine of Cuba and up to and including the use of force to carry out the quarantine if necessary. This seems to me to be a stronger position in support of the United States than that taken by your government."[24]

Not happy with Diefenbaker's attitude during the Cuban Missile Crisis, John F. Kennedy worked to replace his minority Conservative government with one led by Pearson's Liberals. According to *Kennedy and Diefenbaker*, "the man Washington really wanted as Canadian Prime Minister was Mike Pearson."[25] A State Department official, Willis Armstrong, described Kennedy's attitude towards the March 1963 Canadian election: "He wanted to intervene and make sure Pearson got elected. It was very evident the president was uptight about the possibility that Pearson might not win."[26] Later Kennedy's Secretary of State Dean Rusk admitted "in a way, Diefenbaker was right, for it was true that we preferred

Mike Pearson."[27] Rusk further explained: "we'd been spoiled by a long association with Mike Pearson. He was as comfortable as an old shoe."[28]

Immediately after the Cuban Missile Crisis, Kennedy helped precipitate the Diefenbaker government's downfall. "In the fall of 1962," notes *Northern Shadows*, "the State Department began to leak insulting references about Diefenbaker to the U.S. and Canadian press."[29] Articles highly critical of the Canadian Prime Minister appeared in the *New York Times*, *Newsweek* and other major US media outlets. On January 3 the outgoing commander of NATO, US General Lauris Norstad, made a surprise visit to Ottawa where he claimed Canada would not be fulfilling her commitments to the north Atlantic alliance if she did not acquire nuclear warheads. Diefenbaker believed the US general came to Canada "at the behest of President Kennedy" to set the table "for Pearson's conversion to the United States nuclear policy."[30] A future prime minister, Pierre Trudeau, concurred. He asked: "Do you think that General Norstad, the former supreme commander of allied forces in Europe, came to Ottawa as a tourist on January 3 to call publicly on the Canadian government to respect its [nuclear] commitments? Do you think it was by chance that Mr. Pearson, in his speech of January 12, was able to quote the authority of General Norstad? Do you think it was inadvertent that, on January 30, the State Department gave a statement to journalists reinforcing Mr. Pearson's claims and crudely accusing Mr. Diefenbaker of lying? ... you believe that it was by coincidence that this series of events ended with the fall of the [Diefenbaker] government on February 5?"[31]

Trudeau and Diefenbaker's accusations need to be understood in light of the close ties between Pearson and

Kennedy, who was responsible for the Bay of Pigs invasion and early US escalation in Vietnam. As opposition leader, Pearson visited Kennedy on a number of occasions. Not wanting to give the Conservatives more ammunition in their campaign to portray him as an "American stooge" and "Yankee slave", Pearson told Kennedy he needed to conceal their visits and the US President went to extraordinary lengths to do so.[32] On one occasion Kennedy asked Pearson if he had a degree from Harvard and Pearson said yes. Then he asked about the Massachusetts Institute of Technology and Pearson said he had an honorary degree from that school as well. The US president then asked about Boston University and Mike said no, so Kennedy got BU to offer Pearson a degree, giving him a reason to travel to Boston as opposition leader where he met Kennedy over a weekend in 1961.[33]

During the 1963 election campaign Kennedy's top pollster, Lou Harris, helped Pearson get elected prime minister.[34] Kennedy backed Harris' move, though he opposed an earlier request for the pollster to help British Labour leader Harold Wilson, which Harris then declined. Since Harris was closely associated with the US president the Liberals called Kennedy's pollster by a pseudonym.[35]

Washington may have aided Pearson's campaign in other ways. Diefenbaker wondered if the CIA was active during the 1963 election while External Affairs Minister Howard Green said a US agent attended a couple of his campaign meetings in B.C.[36]

To Washington's delight, immediately after Pearson became prime minister, Canada's nuclear policy changed. *US Nuclear Weapons in Canada* reports: "the Liberal [Pearson] government was much more accommodating to the US military than the Conservative Diefenbaker government had been since 1957."[37] Pearson secured nuclear warheads for Honest John missiles as well as CF-101 and CF-104 jets. The foreign stationed CF-104 Starfighter operated without a gun and carried nothing but a thermal nuclear weapon (MK 28 bomb).[38] Most controversially, Pearson's government brought nuclear-armed Bomarc missiles to Canada, which prompted Pierre Trudeau to call Pearson the "defrocked priest of peace".[39]

Pearson's government gave Washington (effective) control over these Canadian nuclear missiles based near North Bay, Ontario. According to the agreement between the two countries, the Canadian battle staff officer on duty would receive authorization from the Colorado Springs based commander in chief of NORAD, "allow[ing] for the release and firing of nuclear armed Bomarc missiles without specific Canadian government authorization."[40]

Again, upon closer inspection, Canada's hero appears less a man of peace than a strident cold warrior.

6. Prime Minister Pearson and Colonialism

In an example of how international affairs are interconnected, Washington's aggressive response to the post-1959 social changes taking place in Cuba, and the resulting Cuban Missile Crisis, brought the nuclear issue to a head in Canada. It also revealed Pearson's active support for imperialist policies and indifference towards colonialism when he was in charge of the government as prime minister.

Pearson, who did business with the Fulgencio Batista dictatorship in Cuba as foreign minister, was more hostile to the post-Batista reforms in Cuba than Diefenbaker. Before the 1963 federal election, Cuban ambassador to Canada, Americo Cruz, cabled Havana his opinion of a Pearson victory. "If the Liberals win the elections the panorama would be gloomier. First because this party has shown itself time and time again to be openly opposed to trading with our country, and has attacked it almost daily in the House. And secondly because if Paul Martin (a sworn enemy of Cuba and the leader of the Catholic community) is named Secretary of State for External Relations, as it is expected, then this will mean that he will be alongside ... that defender of the United States, Mr. Pearson as Prime Minister. [If that were to happen] relations with Cuba, and with all socialist countries, would suffer a most radical change."[1]

Cruz was correct in assuming that a Pearson-led Canada would be more hostile to Cuba. In his first post-election meeting with President Kennedy, the Prime Minister indicated "that the Canadian government would do or say nothing to show support for the Castro government."[2] His government, notes *Canada-Cuba Relations,* "sought to dissuade any initiatives to foster or improve bilateral relations [with Cuba]."[3] Talking points for a December 1963 NATO ministerial meeting suggest the extreme nature of his government's attitude towards Cuba. "The Canadian government, of course, holds no sympathy for the present dictatorial regime in Cuba, which has betrayed the Cuban Revolution's original objectives of liberal social and political reforms and has reduced Cuba to the status of an economically backward police-state dependent upon the Soviet bloc ... we remain deeply disturbed by the presence in the Western Hemisphere of a communist regime aligned with the Soviet Union and by the transformation of Cuba into an area which still retains a potential for disturbing East-West relations and the stability of the Hemisphere."[4]

Pearson supported Washington's policy in the hemisphere and allied Canada more closely with the US in the region. With anti-American sentiment running high after Washington sponsored the April 1961 Bay of Pigs invasion of Cuba, Pearson, leader of the opposition, told a northern Brazil audience: "I beg of you, my Latin American friends, be careful; but don't misjudge the Americans. They are a wonderful and generous people, the least imperialistically minded people that ever had world power thrust on them."[5]

In *Northern Shadows* Peter McFarlane writes that after the new prime minister met Kennedy in May 1963 he brought this country into greater alignment with US policy in the Americas. "All of Canada's Latin American trade commissioners were recalled to Ottawa for consultation and Canada was quietly joining the [US led] Alliance for Progress Inter-American Development Bank."[6] In the fall of that year the government announced "a further contribution to Latin American development, in close co-operation with the Inter-American Development bank."[7] The Alliance for Progress was the Kennedy administration's social-economic response to the excitement created in Latin America by the Cuban revolution. It was designed partly to isolate Cuba from the region. Pearson also thought it would help Canadian businesses.

A year after Prime Minister Pearson met Kennedy, Brazil's military overthrew the country's elected government. Washington backed the coup against President João Goulart. At one point President Lyndon Johnson urged Ambassador Lincoln Gordon to take "every step that we can" to support Goulart's removal. In a declassified cable between Gordon and Washington, the ambassador in Brasília acknowledged US involvement in "covert support for pro-democracy street rallies ... and encouragement [of] democratic and anti-communist sentiment in Congress, armed forces, friendly labor and student groups, church, and business."[8]

Pearson failed to publicly condemn the ouster of Goulart. "The Canadian reaction to the military coup of 1964 was careful, polite and allied with American rhetoric," notes *Brazil and Canada in the Americas*.[9] Washington, Ottawa and leading segments of Brazil's business community opposed Goulart's Reformas de Base (basic reforms). Goulart wanted to expand suffrage by giving illiterates and low ranking military officers the vote. He also wanted to put 15% of the national income into education and to implement land reform. To pay for this the government planned to introduce a proportional income tax and greater controls on the profit transfers of multinational corporations.

As important as following Washington's lead, Pearson's tacit support for the coup was driven by Canadian corporate interests. Among the biggest firms in Latin America at the time, Brascan was commonly known as the "the Canadian octopus" since its tentacles reached into so many areas of Brazil's economy. A study of the Toronto-based company noted "[Brazilian Traction's vice-president Antonio] Gallotti doesn't hide his participation in the moves and operations that led to the coup d'état against Goulart in 1964."[10] Just prior to the coup against Goulart, Brazilian Traction president Grant Glassco remarked "more and more, the various agencies of the government were infiltrated by extremists, many of whom were Communist inspired and directed."[11] After the elected government was overthrown, Glassco stated "the new government of Brazil is ... made up of men of proven competence and integrity. The President, Humberto Castello Branco, commands the respect of the entire nation."[12]

Putting a stop to the Goulart government, which made it more difficult for companies to export profits, was good business.[13] After the 1964 coup the *Financial Post* noted "the price of Brazilian Traction common shares almost doubled overnight with the change of government from an April 1 low of $1.95 to an April 3 high of $3.06."[14] Between 1965 and 1974, Brascan drained Brazil of $342 million ($2 billion today).[15] When Brascan's Canadian president, Robert Winters, was asked why the company's profits grew so rapidly in the late 1960s his response was simple: "The Revolution."[16]

Lester Pearson's Peacekeeping

Before he took charge of Brascan Winters was Pearson's trade minister. Similarly, Jack Nicholson, a Brazilian Traction chief executive in Brazil in the 1950s, held a number of cabinet positions in the Pearson government.[17] Long-time Liberal civil servant, Mitchell Sharp, went from deputy minister in the Department of Trade and Commerce to vice-president of Brascan. A year before the coup Mike appointed him finance minister.

The year after Goulart was overthrown Pearson also supported the US invasion of the Dominican Republic. At the end of 1962 Juan Bosch won the country's first clean election. After three decades of the Rafael Trujillo dictatorship, Bosch encouraged civil society by training co-operative, union and peasant leaders. The Dominican President also moved to break up some of the country's large plantations and pushed constitutional changes that expanded the rights of labour, women and children. After seven months in office Bosch was exiled in a military coup backed by large landowners, the church and industrialists. With Washington's support, the elected government was replaced by a three-man military junta. Growing dissatisfaction with the coup regime spurred a counter military rebellion by "constitutionalist" forces demanding Bosch be restored to office. After the coup regime was removed from power, the US intervened. At the end of April 1965 more than 20,000 US troops were sent to the Dominican Republic. In response to the invasion, Pearson told Parliament: "the United States government has intervened in the Dominican Republic for the protection of its own citizens and those of other countries."[18] Asked whether the "United States has the right to violate the sovereign rights of the Dominican Republic by the landing of marines?" the Prime Minister said: "I think it is well known in international law — indeed it is accepted in the Organization of

American States — that a government has the responsibility for protecting its own people in situations of insurrection and disturbance when those citizens are in danger and when the forces of law and order seem to have temporarily disappeared."[19]

The government continued to defend US actions even after it became abundantly clear that Washington was not simply protecting US civilians. Three weeks after the US deployed its troops an NDP Member of Parliament referred to the "invasion of this Republic by the United States", prompting Pearson's external minister to complain about this "extravagant characterization" of "the American interest in Latin America and the Dominican Republic."[20] Ottawa rejected a request by "constitutionalist" General Francisco Caamaño, appointed president until Bosch could return, for diplomatic recognition. In explaining his decision Pearson told Parliament "there are indeed communists in the directing group who are controlling that particular ... group seeking recognition."[21]

While a Canadian warship in the Caribbean was sent "to stand by in case it is required", a few Latin American countries sent troops to participate in an Organization of American States mission designed to relieve US troops from the country. [22] On May 28 Pearson told the House: "I am sure we would all wish to see this [OAS] force carry out successfully its functions of bringing peace and stability to the Dominican Republic."[23]

A year after invading, the US set up "demonstration elections" won by a former Trujillo official, Joaquin Belaguer. The Pearson government supported Belaguer with one of its first bilateral grants to a Latin American country. Canada gave $298,000 in food aid to the Dominican Republic in 1966 as part of the "mop-up in the wake of the 1965 military invasion of that country."[24]

Ottawa supported the US invasion partly out of concern for Canadian investments in the Dominican. Just after the US intervened the external minister told Parliament, "We have ... been in touch by telephone with the Falconbridge Nickel plant ... and we are told that all is well in that quarter."[25] Later he said "the embassy is also investigating reports that the main branch of the Royal Bank of Canada has been looted."[26] Concern for Canadian corporate assets was driven by the size of the investments. At the time of the invasion Canadian banking interests held nearly 70 percent of the Dominican's foreign-owned banking assets.[27] Falconbridge's interests in the Dominican were not insignificant either and the US intervention was good for business. The year after the invasion Falconbridge quadrupled the size of its experimental pilot plant in the country. By 1972 this viciously antiunion employer controlled the single largest foreign investment in the country.

While some corporations benefited other Canadians objected to the government's moves. *Our Place in the Sun* explains: "the PCM [progressive church movement] excoriated the government of Lester B. Pearson for having supported the US invasion of the Dominican Republic."[28]

A year after the invasion of the Dominican Republic the Pearson government once again sent warships to the Caribbean. Two Canadian gunboats were deployed to Barbados's 1966 independence celebration in a bizarre diplomatic maneuver designed to demonstrate Canada's military prowess. *Canadian Gunboat Diplomacy* explains: "We can only speculate at who the 'signal' was directed towards, but given the fact that tensions were running high in the Caribbean over the Dominican Republic Affair [the US invasion], it is likely that the targets were any outside force, probably Cuban, which might be tempted to interfere with

Barbadian independence."[29] Of course Canadian naval vessels were considered no threat to Barbadian independence.[30] Intervening in another country to defend it from possible outside intervention may be the pinnacle of the imperial mindset.

Both this mindset and the resulting Canadian actions were noted by some nationalist Caribbean leaders. In February 1966 Pearson announced that Canada, Trinidad and Jamaica hoped to organize a conference to promote regional economic cooperation. The Prime Minister of British Guyana, Forbes Burnham, replied that he did not want to participate in a conference led by Canadians since it was "time Caribbean countries stopped running to conferences called by outsiders."[31]

Perhaps Pearson's accommodating attitude towards South African racism was also noticed in the Caribbean. As opposition leader Pearson continued to demonstrate a certain amount of sympathy for the apartheid regime. When African and Asian countries (and ultimately the Diefenbaker government) pushed South Africa to leave the Commonwealth in 1961, Pearson said he took "no satisfaction out of this withdrawal."[32] Then during his term as prime minister the South African regime's repression continued unabated. Sentenced to life in prison in 1964, Nelson Mandela, leader of the African National Congress, joined 1,500 black political activists languishing in South African jails.[33] In June 1964 NDP leader Tommy Douglas told the House: "Nelson Mandela and seven of his associates have been found guilty of contravening the apartheid laws ... [I] ask the Prime Minister if he will make vigorous representation to the government of South Africa urging that they exercise clemency in this case"? Pearson responded that the "eight defendants ... have been found guilty on charges of sabotage and conspiracy ... While the matter is still sub judice [before the courts] it would, I believe, be improper for the government to make any public statement on the verdict or on the possible sentences."[34] This author found no follow up comment by Pearson regarding Mandela.

Unperturbed by the racist and repressive regime, one book notes how the Prime Minister "stubbornly defended" economic ties to South Africa.[35] Despite criticism from the NDP, *Ambiguous Champion* notes "[Pearson] placed no restrictions on Canadian economic relations with South Africa, not even on official promotion of trade and investment."[36] With South Africa leaving the Commonwealth Tommy Douglas asked if the government was "giving thought to discontinuing the Commonwealth [economic] preferences which we now extend to that country?" Pearson replied: "No immediate consideration is being given to that matter."[37] In November 1963 Ottawa also failed to support a widely endorsed General Assembly resolution calling for an oil embargo against South Africa.[38]

The refusal to sever business relations with the apartheid regime was largely motivated by economic interests but it was also tied to the Pearson government's racist worldview. In a speech largely critical of apartheid, Pearson's foreign minister accepted a central element of the white regime's racist justification. In November 1963 he told the House: "The Canadian government can understand the fears of White South Africans about being submerged and eventually forced out of their homeland."[39]

Pearson's willingness to accept colonialism and racism is also shown by his attitude towards another white supremacist regime. In the mid-1960s the white minority in South Africa's northern neighbour Rhodesia (now Zimbabwe) unilaterally declared independence from Britain on explicitly racist terms.

Despite the white regime's lack of a one-person one-vote system of majority rule, Ottawa failed to enforce UN sanctions against Rhodesia. Falconbridge, for instance, maintained its Rhodesian subsidiary, which continued normal relations with the Canadian head office. In September 1966 Pearson opposed an African proposal for blanket UN sanctions on Rhodesia and South Africa.[40] He said these conditions "would tie that country to South Africa, and would link a satisfactory solution of the Rhodesian problem with a long and difficult economic siege of South Africa."[41] African governments were far from enthused with Canada's position on Rhodesia. *Ambiguous Champion* explains: "To shift attention from the unpalatable aspects of this stance, Pearson pledged Canadian support for a program of assistance in the form of scholarships for Rhodesian Africans and capital assistance for Rhodesian railways and irrigation."[42] Ottawa also gave African countries assistance to ease tension between them and the leader of the Commonwealth, Britain, which empowered the white minority in Rhodesia.[43]

Pearson resisted African and Asian countries' more forthright criticism of Rhodesian racism. He did, however, concede to some of their demands. To avoid a split within the organization on racial lines he supported a July 1964 Commonwealth statement on racial equality and non-discrimination.[44] Pearson believed some concessions were needed to preempt an African exodus from the Commonwealth and Western sphere.

During his time as prime minister Portugal waged brutal wars against liberation movements in its colonies of Angola, Mozambique and Guinea Bissau. Thousands were killed in fighting that raged for nearly a decade. Rather than work to undermine Portuguese colonialism, Canada expanded its economic ties to the colonies.[45] Canadian trade officials busied themselves promoting the incentives Portugal offered in its "overseas provinces."[46] Pearson's government opposed UN resolutions calling upon members to stop trading with Portugal and investing in its colonies. On December 5, 1966, for instance, Canada voted against a UN resolution calling for self-determination in the Portuguese territories. Ottawa objected because the resolution called for mandatory action.[47] Similarly, when the General Assembly voted 75 to 12 (with 16 abstentions) to condemn financial interests active in the Portuguese territories Pearson's government opposed the resolution.[48] In supporting Portugal, Ottawa ignored both international and domestic opinion. An internal External Affairs file noted, in June 1968, "a vocal segment of the Canadian public has recently been critical of the government's continuing reluctance to adopt a clearer policy towards Portuguese colonialism."[49]

Canada's complicity with Portuguese colonialism went beyond diplomatic and economic support. Ottawa also provided military assistance to the Portuguese. On a number of occasions Canadian technologies were found in Portuguese armaments, including parts made by Computing Devices of Canada and Aviation Ltd in the wreckage of a Fiat G-91 fighter, shot down in Guinea Bissau.[50] Ottawa saw no problem with NATO weapons going to Portugal.[51]

While Angola, Mozambique and Guinea Bissau struggled for their independence in the mid-60s, the first African country to win its freedom from Britain found itself under foreign pressure. In February 1966 Ghana's Canadian-trained army overthrew President Kwame Nkrumah, a leading Pan-Africanist. Dubbed "Man of the Millennium" in a 2000 poll by BBC listeners in Africa, Nkrumah pursued state-centric socialistic policies and co-founded the Non-Aligned Movement. Washington and London backed the coup against Nkrumah.[52] While direct ties between Canadian military trainers and those responsible for Nkrumah's ouster have yet to be documented, Pearson's government definitely gave its blessing to the coup. *The Deceptive Ash* explains: "The Western orientation and the more liberal approach of the new military government was welcomed by Canada."[53] Just after Nkrumah was overthrown, Canada sent $1.82 million worth of flour to Ghana and offered the military regime a hundred CUSO volunteers.[54] Despite severing financial assistance to Nkrumah's government, immediately after the coup the IMF restructured Ghana's debt. Canada's contribution was an outright gift.[55] From 1966 to 1969 the National Liberation Council, the military regime, received as much aid as during Nkrumah's ten years in office. Ottawa gave $22 million in grants and loans, the fourth major donor after the US, UK and UN.[56] Canada provided diplomatic support for the coup as well. The day Nkrumah was overthrown Pearson was asked his opinion about this development. He said nothing of substance on the matter. The next day External Affairs Minister Paul Martin responded to questions about Canada's military training in Ghana by saying there was no change in instructions. In response to a question about recognizing the military government Martin said: "In many cases recognition is accorded automatically. In respective cases such as that which occurred in Ghana yesterday, the practice is developing of carrying on with the government which is taken over, but according no formal act until some interval has elapsed. We shall carry on with the present arrangement for Ghana. Whether there will be any formal act will depend on information which is not now before us."[57]

Less than two weeks after the coup the Pearson government told the military junta that Canada intended to carry on normal relations.[58] Six months after overthrowing Nkrumah, the coup's leader, General Joseph Ankrah, made an official visit to Ottawa as part of a trip that also took him through London and Washington.[59]

A year after Nkrumah was overthrown, Canadian soldiers were forced unceremoniously from another African country. On May 28, 1967 Canada's 800-man contingent was ordered to leave Egypt within 48 hours. In the lead-up to Israel's June 5 invasion, Pearson blamed that country's neighbours for rising regional tensions. Ignoring Israel's raids into Syria and the Jordanian-occupied West Bank, he told Parliament on May 24: "The basic issue in this situation, it seems to me … is the recognition of Israel's right to live in peace and security. The rejection and repudiation of that basic right has been over the years and is now a source of our danger. It is not the immediate manifestation of that danger but it certainly is a source of it. So long as Israel's neighbors, or some of them, refuse to recognize the right of Israel to exist as a state, then we move from one crisis to another. Israel, of course, also has the basic obligation, which I am sure she accepts, to live without provocations and threats to her neighbors and in accord with United Nations' resolutions which gave her birth."[60]

Canada co-sponsored (with Denmark) an emergency Security Council meeting to call attention to Egypt's blockade of Israeli shipping through the Strait of Tiran on the Gulf of Aqaba. Undermining UN Secretary General U Thant's efforts to reduce tension, Ottawa made this move while the head of the UN negotiated the issue with President Nasser in Cairo. The emergency meeting contributed to the sense of crisis, which Israel used to justify invading Egypt. Ottawa also supported a British and American proposal to establish a maritime force to protect Israeli shipping through the Strait of Tiran. On May 26, 1967 Pearson told Parliament he was "in complete agreement" with US President Lyndon Johnson on the "importance of maintaining the right of access to and innocent passage through the Gulf of Aqaba, and that everything possible should be done through the United Nations to see if this can be arranged."[61]

Made during a politically turbulent time, the Egyptians considered Ottawa's comments and actions a threat. In response to Canada's aggressive posture, Nasser expelled Canadian troops and public protests took place at the Canadian Chancellery building in Egypt. Radio Cairo called Pearson a "silly idiot" while *Al Ahram* newspaper wrote that Canada was "a stooge of the Western powers who seek to colonize the Arab world with Israel's help."[62]

Canada, Britain and the US exaggerated the importance of Egypt's blockade of Israeli shipping through the Strait of Tiran. Ignoring any sense of proportion, Pearson told the House on May 24 that the "Gulf of Aqaba now is of vital importance to the existence of the state of Israel."[63] But, Iranian oil shipments were the only important commodity affected by Egypt's blockade and they could be rerouted to the Israeli city of Haifa. More generally, Harvard Law Professor Roger Fisher explains: "The United Arab Republic [Egypt] had a good legal case for restricting traffic through the Straits of Tiran. First, it is debatable whether international law confers any rights of innocent passage through such a waterway. Despite an Israeli request, the International Law Commission in 1956 found no rule which would govern the Straits of Tiran. Although the 1958 convention on the Territorial Sea does provide for innocent passage through such straits, the United States Representative, Arthur Dean, called this 'a new rule' and U.A.R. has not signed the treaty. There are, of course, good arguments on the Israeli side too, and an impartial international court might well conclude that the right of innocent passage through the Straits of Tiran does exist. But a right of innocent passage is not a right of free passage for any cargo at any time. In the words of the convention on the Territorial Sea: 'passage is innocent so long as it is not prejudicial to the peace, good order or security of the coastal states.' In April Israel conducted major retaliatory raids on Syria [which had a mutual defence agreement with Egypt] and threatened raids of still greater size. In this situation was Egypt required by international law to continue to allow Israel to bring oil and other strategic supplies through Egyptian territory — supplies which Israel could use to conduct further military raids? That was the critical question of law."[64]

Egypt's blockade of Israeli shipping garnered greater attention than it deserved while Israeli (and American) geo-strategic aims were downplayed. According to a CIA analysis just before the June 1967 war, Israel's goals were "(1) Destruction of the center of power of the radical Arab Socialist movement, i.e. the Nasser regime. (2) Destruction of the arms of the radical Arabs. (3) Destruction of both Syria and Jordan as modern states."[65]

Alongside Washington, Pearson apparently supported these objectives. Additionally, the Saudi monarchy, a major oil producer and important US ally, was under increasing pressure from Nasser-led Pan-Arabism. Egypt and Saudi Arabia were fighting a proxy war in North Yemen in support of Arab nationalist and royalist factions, respectively. The Saudis definitely benefited from Israel's attack against Egypt.

When Israel invaded Egypt on June 5 Pearson told Parliament: "This is not the time to establish responsibility, let alone assess blame for what happened in the early hours of this morning."⁶⁶ Three days later he endorsed Israel's military gains. "To bring the Israeli forces back behind the borders of last week, without doing anything about the situation in the Gulf of Aqaba, would not provide for peace but merely a temporary absence of hostilities."⁶⁷ That same day External Affairs Minister Paul Martin publically lauded "the brave people of Israel."⁶⁸

After the war Canada continued to defend Israeli policy. Even though Israel won in six days Pearson implied that it faced an Arab Goliath. In a memo he wrote: "I agree that Israel is entitled to far stronger international guarantees of security than she has had in the past. I believe that Israel has the right to use her present strong position to bargain to this end."⁶⁹ On June 16, he told Parliament Israel's withdrawal from the territories it conquered during the war (Egypt's Sinai, Syria's Golan Heights, Gaza and the West Bank) "should be accompanied by effective international guarantees of security of Israel."⁷⁰

Following through on this statement, Canada voted against a Yugoslav resolution calling for Israel to withdraw behind the armistice lines and for the secretary-general to consider remaining questions immediately after Israel's withdrawal. Author Ali Dessouki explains: "Canada has to recognize the inconsistency between its policy in May prior to the hostilities, and its policy after the Israeli victory. Prior to the hostilities, Canada's view was that no progress in negotiations could take place unless the Gulf of Aqaba were reopened to Israeli shipping thereby restoring the status quo ante. Following the Israeli victory Canada adopted an entirely different position. Now, restoration of the status quo, i.e., withdrawal of Israeli forces together with international guarantees of Israeli shipping rights, must be accompanied by a political settlement of all major issues."⁷¹

Lester Pearson's Peacekeeping

Ottawa actively supported Israel before, during and after the 1967 war. During that war tens of thousands of Syrians were expelled from the Golan Heights and between 200,000 and 250,000 Palestinians were driven out of the West Bank (17,000 were allowed to return).[72] On two different occasions Pearson and Paul Martin were queried in the House about these expulsions and both times they said they'd take the question as notice. A week after the ceasefire agreement Pearson was asked about Egyptian soldiers, previously attacked by Israeli forces, dying of thirst in the Sinai. He responded: "The Israeli authorities are taking all possible steps to avert human suffering. ... the government in occupation of these territories is doing whatever it can to meet this terrible problem."[73] Three months after the conclusion of hostilities Israel began setting up illegal settlements in the West Bank.[74] The 1967 war led to Israel's now over four decade-long occupation of the West Bank, Gaza, East Jerusalem and Golan Heights.

7. The Case for War Crime Charges

As outlined earlier, Pearson consistently supported Washington's aggressive attempts to block East Asian nationalism. This continued through his time as prime minister and, one could argue, escalated into actively supporting activities best described as war crimes.

What is a war crime? Canada's Crimes Against Humanity and War Crimes Act states: "War crime means an act or omission committed during an armed conflict that, at the time and in the place of its commission, constitutes a war crime according to customary international law or conventional international law applicable to armed conflicts, whether or not it constitutes a contravention of the law in force at the time and in the place of its commission." The Rome Treaty creating the International Criminal Court defined war crimes as follows (the most relevant clauses):

"(a) Grave breaches of the Geneva Conventions of 12 August 1949, namely, any of the following acts against persons or property protected under the provisions of the relevant Geneva Convention:

"(i) Wilful killing; (ii) Torture or inhuman treatment, including biological experiments; (iii) Wilfully causing great suffering, or serious injury to body or health; (iv) Extensive destruction and appropriation of property, not justified by military necessity and carried out unlawfully and wantonly ...

"(b) Other serious violations of the laws and customs applicable in international armed conflict, within the established framework of international law, namely, any of the following acts:

"(i) Intentionally directing attacks against the civilian population as such or against individual civilians not taking direct part in hostilities; (ii) Intentionally directing attacks against civilian objects, that is, objects which are not military objectives ... (iv) Intentionally launching an attack in the knowledge that such attack will cause incidental loss of life or injury to civilians or damage to civilian objects or widespread, long-term and severe damage to the natural environment which would be clearly excessive in relation to the concrete and direct overall military advantage anticipated; (v) Attacking or bombarding, by whatever means, towns, villages, dwellings or buildings which are undefended and which are not military objectives ... (viii) The transfer, directly or indirectly, by the Occupying Power of parts of its own civilian population into the territory it occupies, or the deportation or transfer of all or parts of the population of the occupied territory within or outside this territory ... (xxv) Intentionally using starvation of civilians as a method of warfare by depriving them of objects indispensable to their survival, including wilfully impeding relief supplies as provided for under the Geneva Conventions ..."[1]

Many respected commentators and legal experts have argued that French, British, Dutch, American and other military campaigns to suppress colonial revolts in Asia during the post World War II era resulted in war crimes. Clearly, as events outlined above and below demonstrate, Pearson generally supported European and American actions and in some cases as prime minister directly enabled activities best described as war crimes. The reader as truth and reconciliation commissioner must decide if Pearson's responsibility in these actions would meet the threshold requirement for a war crime charge.

As outlined in the Foreword by Noam Chomsky, Pearson's role in enabling the bombing of North Vietnam is the reason some people consider him a war criminal. But to truly understand what was happening in Vietnam, one must widen the lens and take a quick look at the wider context in East Asia at the time. Colonial powers and their local supporters were quite willing to use extreme force and brutality to get their way.

In a bid to maintain its influence in East Asia, in mid-1961 London pushed to merge its colonies of North Borneo, Sarawak and Singapore with Malaya (technically independent from England since 1957) to create Malaysia. Independent Indonesia objected to what it saw as a subservient Malaysian government's willingness to extend colonial authority on its border. Conflict between Indonesia and Malaysia escalated into a low-level war.

Pearson sided with the Malaysian leader Tunku. During a visit to Ottawa by Tunku Pearson said "under his leadership the peoples of Malaysia have been brought closer together in freedom, democracy and greater human welfare" despite Indonesian "pressure dedicated to their destruction."[2] *Fire and the Full Moon* notes: "Ottawa avoided direct military involvement but was clearly a partisan and on the Malaysian side."[3] In the midst of the conflict, the Liberal government cut a small disbursement of food aid to Indonesia while releasing $4 million ($28 million today) in military aid to Malaysia.[4] In response, Indonesian President Sukarno added Canada to his list of "imperialists with white skins", which included the US, New Zealand, Australia and

Britain.⁵ A nationalist Indonesian newspaper, *Suluh*, said Ottawa should "go to hell."⁶

An External Affairs assessment of Indonesian foreign policy during this period concluded that Sukarno wanted "an endless succession of foreign adventures" to satisfy his "personal and national megalomania."⁷ Canada's ambassador in Jakarta further explained: "He [Sukarno] wants revolutionary change in the balance of economic power between the developed and less developed nations ... We believe that under Sukarno Indonesia is already a lost cause as far as the free world is concerned."⁸

Sukarno's aggressive opposition to British policy in Malaysia hastened a slow moving US-backed military takeover, which included the eventual slaughter of 500,000 Indonesian "communists". Enabled by external and internal dynamics, in late 1965 Major General Suharto oversaw a wave of terror that left hundreds of thousands of landless peasants and Communist Party members dead.⁹ Suharto, Commander of the Army Strategic Reserve, then overthrew democratically elected president Sukarno. In the lead-up to this bloody military coup, the US government authorized a covert program in late 1964 to assist the "good men in the government, armed services and the private sector" who might topple Sukarno if Washington supported their efforts.¹⁰ Washington also worked to paint the Communist Party of Indonesia (PKI) as an agent of China and enemy of Indonesian nationalism.

Pearson's government backed the Indonesian general's repressive political machinations. Even though he was aware of Suharto's killing, in early 1966 Canada's ambassador in Jakarta called this mass murderer "a moderate, sensible and progressive leader."¹¹ An External Affairs memorandum explained: "Changes in the political orientation of Indonesia have already had a profound effect on the prospects for stability in South East Asia. It is patently in our interests that the new [Suharto] regime be able to consolidate its internal position and to pursue external policies it appears prepared to follow. These are policies which promise to make the situation much easier not only for the smaller countries of the area but also for Australia, New Zealand, the UK and the USA."[12]

To aid Suharto Ottawa selected Indonesia as the main Asian country outside of the Commonwealth to receive Canadian aid.[13] *Rain Dancing* explains: "The domestic political stability achieved by Suharto after the ouster of Sukarno in 1966, together with a pronounced tilt in foreign policy towards the West, made Indonesia an attractive target in the eyes of [Canadian] policymakers."[14] Ottawa preferred Suharto's Western-trained technocrats to Sukarno's anti-colonial nationalism.[15] "Only with the removal of Sukarno from power," notes *Fire and Full Moon*, "would the Government of Canada smile on Indonesia again."[16]

The coup in Indonesia took place as war raged in the southern part of Vietnam. In 1965 over 100,000 US troops were defending an unpopular dictatorship in the South and by 1968 that number peaked at half a million. As many as three million Vietnamese were killed in 20 years of fighting.[17]

To undermine the rural based Viet Minh's power the US military drove peasants from the South Vietnamese countryside. "The massacre of the rural population of Vietnam and their forced evacuation is not an accidental by-product of the war", Noam Chomsky explained at the time. "Rather it is of the very essence of American strategy."[18] US troops perpetrated innumerable massacres, most infamously in the village of Mai Lai where between 347 and 504 defenceless civilians were slaughtered.[19]

Though less publicized, dozens of massacres similar to the one in Mai Lai took place during the war.[20] Additionally, in a five-year operation known as the Phoenix Program, CIA officers, US special operation forces and South Vietnamese security personnel assassinated tens of thousands of Vietnamese without trial.[21]

The US air campaign was also deadly. Historian Howard Zinn writes: "By the end of the Vietnam war, seven million tons of bombs had been dropped on Vietnam, more than twice the bombs dropped on Europe and Asia in World War II — almost one five-hundred-pound bomb for every human being in Vietnam."[22] Laos and Cambodia were also not spared from US bombing.

"The Pearson Government", notes *Partner to Behemoth,* "frankly supported all the aims of US policy in Vietnam."[23] The prime minister made innumerable declarations in support of US policy. My government, he told Parliament in the spring of 1965, "supports the purposes and objectives of United States policy in Vietnam."[24] On another occasion he said: "This government had supported the policy of the United States in Vietnam and wished to continue that support."[25] Canada's eminent statesman claimed North Vietnam was responsible for the US war in the south. "North Viet Nam has been the aggressor since that country was divided. Let us not forget that fact."[26] After widespread domestic and international condemnation of the war Pearson continued to defend US policy. In May 1967 he told the House: "I believe that the United States moved into Vietnam in the first place to help South Vietnam, at the invitation of the government of that country, to defend itself against military action and subversive terrorism aimed at preventing the people of that part of Vietnam making their own decision as to their future development and political institutions rather than having one particular solution forced upon them under the guise of a liberation struggle conducted in the interests of a totalitarian communist regime in North Vietnam which has not allowed and does not intend to allow its own people any choice as to their social, economic or political system."[27]

Quiet Complicity summarizes the government's position: "Ottawa denied the indigenous character of the struggle, accused Hanoi [North Vietnam] of aggression, subscribed to the Domino theory, blamed Beijing for the popular insurrections in South East Asia, white washed the regime in Saigon [South Vietnam], and absolved it of its responsibilities towards the Geneva Accords, and invoked article 51 of the United Nations charter to exonerate the United States."[28]

Despite the preponderance of evidence suggesting otherwise, Pearson is often portrayed as an opponent of the war. An April 1965 speech he delivered at Temple University in Philadelphia is probably the most often cited example of a Canadian leader (supposedly) opposing US militarism. Linda McQuaig, for instance, cites it glowingly in *Holding the Bully's Coat*, claiming "one could argue that Pearson's urgings may have, in some small way, contributed to ending the U.S. war effort in Vietnam."[29] (To be precise McQuaig's quote refers to Pearson's Temple speech and a private meeting he had with LBJ two years later.)

If similar statements had not been made elsewhere, McQuaig's comment would be hard to fathom. Here's part of what Pearson said in Philadelphia: "The government and great majority of people of my country have supported wholeheartedly the US peacekeeping and peacemaking policies in Vietnam."[30] In *Quiet Complicity*, a book McQuaig cites, Victor Levant puts Pearson's Temple speech (available online) in proper context: "In his Temple speech, the Prime Minister did accept all the premises and almost all the conclusions of US policy. The chief cause of the escalation of the war in Vietnam, in Pearson's view, was North Vietnamese aggression. 'This situation cannot be expected to improve,' he said, 'until North Vietnam becomes convinced that aggression, in whatever guise, for whatever reason, is inadmissible and will not succeed.' This had wider implications, since 'no nation... could ever feel secure if capitulation in Vietnam led to the sanctification of aggression through subversion and spurious wars of national liberation.' If peace was to be achieved, the first condition was a cease-fire, and this could happen only if Hanoi recognizes the error of its ways: 'aggressive action by North Vietnam to bring about a Communist liberation (which means Communist rule) of the South must end. Only then can there be negotiations.' Since US military action was aimed at resisting Hanoi's aggression, the measures taken so far, including the bombing of the North, were entirely justified: 'the retaliatory strikes against North Vietnamese military targets, for which there has been great provocation, aim at making it clear that the maintenance of aggressive policies toward the south will become increasingly costly to the northern regime. After about two months of airstrikes, the message should now have been received loud and clear.'"

Levant continues: "On the other hand, Pearson argued that continued bombing, instead of weakening Hanoi's will to resist, might have the effect of driving it into an even more intransigent position. He therefore suggested, as a tactical move, that the United States consider a carefully timed 'pause' in the bombing: 'there are many factors which I am not in a position to weigh. But there does appear to be at least a possibility that a suspension of such airstrikes against North Vietnam, at the right time, might provide the Hanoi authorities with an opportunity, if they wish to take it, to inject some flexibility into their policy without appearing to do so as the direct result of military pressure. If such a suspension took place for a limited time, then the rate of incidents in South Vietnam would provide a fairly accurate way of measuring its usefulness and the desirability of continuing. I am not, of course, proposing any compromise on points of principle, nor any weakening of resistance to aggression in South Vietnam. Indeed, resistance may require increased military strength to be used against the armed and attacking Communists. I merely suggest that a measured and announced pause in one field of military action at the right time might facilitate the development of diplomatic resources which cannot easily be applied to the problem under the existing circumstances. It could, at the least, expose the intransigence of the North Vietnam government.'"[31]

Let's further dissect Pearson's "anti-war" position. Approximately three million Vietnamese died during the US war in Indochina, about 100,000 of whom were killed during the US bombing of the North. To put Pearson's Temple speech in the crassest terms possible, opposing the bombing of the North was a call to end 3.3% of the death toll.

The day after he spoke in Philadelphia, President Lyndon Johnson privately berated the Canadian Prime Minister, a story Pearson's supporters describe in (probably exaggerated) detail. Johnson was mad because senior US foreign-policy planners were debating a pause in the bombing of North Vietnam and Pearson effectively sided with Johnson's opponents in the US administration after he enabled the bombing campaign (see below). In fact, Pearson told friend and journalist Bruce Hutchison that a highly placed US government official told him to speak out on the bombing of North Vietnam.[32]

Struck by Johnson's anger, Pearson wrote the president to apologize. "I want to assure you that my government, and I particularly as its leader, want to give you all possible support in the policy, difficult and thankless, you are following in Vietnam in aiding South Vietnam to resist aggression. I believe that the great majority of the Canadian people feel the same way."[33]

At the end of 1965 the US halted its bombing of the North for a month. After Washington resumed its actions in the new year, Pearson justified the bombing. He told Parliament "that [North Vietnamese] government was completely intransigent in so far as entering into negotiations was concerned."[34] Six months later the US escalated its bombing in major northern cities. Queried about this development Pearson replied: "The United States does not regard the bombing of oil storage installations in the vicinity of Hanoi and Haiphong as any indication of a change in their policy of confining the bombing to military targets directly associated with North Vietnam's involvement in the south."[35] Ten months later he was asked whether the government had expressed its opposition to the US "bombing inside [the] territory of Haiphong"? Pearson replied, "No, Mr. Speaker, I have made no protest, nor would I even consider doing so until I had detailed information as to the nature of this particular operation."[36] He repeated this position before the House five days later.

The Prime Minister's support for the US war increasingly found him at odds with public opinion and his own cabinet. *Pearson: the Unlikely Gladiator* notes: "During Pearson's final year in office, Canada's approach to the crisis in Southeast Asia reflected the Prime Minister's cautious determination to maintain harmonious relations with Washington. In the face of pressure from the Canadian public and Cabinet, Pearson refused to condemn American policy ... When [Minister] Walter Gordon urged [External Affairs Minister, Paul] Martin and Pearson to press the US to halt the bombing in May 1967, Pearson rebuked him in public."[37]

The Prime Minister provided more than just ideological support for the US intervention in South East Asia. Millions of dollars in Canadian aid, mostly through the Free World Assistance Program, was delivered to support the brutal South Vietnamese regime. The former administrator of the Canadian aid program, Liberal MP David Anderson, admitted to an External Affairs Committee in December 1968 that "a good portion of our aid was strictly for political purposes that were of no value to the people in the area concerned."[38] *Quiet Complicity* notes: "Canadian aid was an integral part of U.S. counter-insurgency efforts aimed at maintaining South Vietnam within the western sphere of influence."[39]

Washington lobbied Ottawa to increase its aid to South Vietnam. On July 26, 1965, for instance, President Johnson wrote Pearson about his plan to increase US forces in Vietnam and requested further Canadian assistance. The Prime Minister was sympathetic.[40] Canadian assistance grew in tandem with US troop numbers. *Quiet Complicity* describes "the pattern which had emerged of increasing Canadian aid paralleling US military escalation."[41]

On two occasions in October 1967 External Affairs Minister Paul Martin boasted to the House that Canada delivered more aid to (south) Vietnam than all but two countries. "Since we began Canadian aid to Vietnam in 1953 we have allocated as much money as any other country but two."[42] Presumably, the US and France were the two countries Martin considered more generous than Canada. By associating Canadian aid with the efforts of these two imperial states, Martin revealed a great deal about External Affairs' definition of aid.

Similar to aid, weapons sales to the US increased alongside the military buildup in Vietnam. Canadian weapons sales to the US doubled between 1964 and 1966, peaking in 1967.[43] During Pearson's time as prime minister, Canada sold hundreds of millions of dollars worth of war materials to the Pentagon, making this country one of the world's leading arms exporters on a per capita basis.[44] *Snow Job* notes: "American planes [that dropped rockets and napalm on North Vietnamese towns or southern villages] were often guided by Canadian made Marconi-Doppler navigation systems and used bombing computers built in Rexdale, Ontario. The bombs could have been armed with dynamite shipped from Valleyfield, Québec; polystyrene, a major component in napalm, was supplied by Dow Chemical. Defoliants came from Naugatuck Chemicals in Elmira, Ontario, and air-to-ground rockets were furnished by the Ingersoll Machine and Tool Company. On the ground, American infantry and artillery units were supplied by De Havilland Caribou built at Milton, Ontario. Less lethal Canadian products included Bata boots for the troops and the famous green berets of the Special Forces which came from Dorothea Knitting Mills in Toronto ... Canadian Arsenals Ltd, a Crown corporation, sold small arms, fill for artillery shells, mines, bombs, grenades, torpedo warheads, depth charges and rockets."[45]

In different periods Pearson either denied or defended these weapon sales. On one occasion he said: "The shipment of Canadian military supplies to Vietnam would be incompatible with our role in the International Control Commission."[46] This highly misleading statement was clearly contradicted by internal discussions. In a September 1965 Cabinet meeting, for instance, Paul Martin "reported that the United States Department of Defense had increased its procurement recently in Canada of a number of items destined for use in Vietnam."[47]

Pushed by a significant protest movement, NDP leader Tommy Douglas urged the Liberals to follow Sweden's example by ending weapons sales to the US until there was peace in Vietnam.[48] Similarly, North Vietnam formally called on Ottawa to halt these weapon sales.[49] In 1967 Pearson responded to calls for Ottawa to end the Defense Production Sharing Arrangements, the agreement under which Canada sold the US weapons, with the claim that to so do would imperil this country's foreign policy. He claimed this "would be interpreted as a notice of withdrawal on our part from continental defense and even from the collective defense arrangements of the Atlantic alliance."[50] In other words, if we stop selling the US weapons for their war in South East Asia Canada would have to pull out of NORAD and NATO and the world, as we know it, will end.

Those who supported continued arm sales often responded to protesters' demands by claiming that Canadian weapons were not central to the US war effort. According to its opponents, a weapons ban would harm Canada's economy while Washington would simply procure armaments elsewhere. This line of argument may have been correct, but it's pretty clear that "Canadian nickel, aluminum, iron ore, and steel were essential to the U.S. war machine." *Snow Job* continues: "It was no coincidence that these exports rose dramatically during the height of the Vietnam conflict in the 1960s."[51]

Canada's abundant resources as well as its vast landmass aided the US military effort in Southeast Asia. B-52 bombers practised bombing runs in Saskatchewan and Alberta while the US tested chemical weapons (agents orange, purple and blue) at CFB Gagetown.[52]

A 1968 US Army memorandum titled "Defoliation Tests in 1966 at base Gagetown, New Brunswick, Canada" explained: "The Department of the Army, Fort Detrick, Maryland, has been charged with finding effective chemical agents that will cause rapid defoliation of woody and Herbaceous vegetation. To further develop these objectives, large areas similar in density to those of interest in South East Asia were needed. In March 1965, the Canadian Ministry of Defense offered Crops Division large areas of densely forested land for experimental tests of defoliant chemicals. This land, located at Canadian Forces Base Gagetown, Oromocto, New Brunswick, was suitable in size and density and was free from hazards and adjacent cropland. The test site selected contained a mixture of conifers and deciduous broad leaf species in a dense undisturbed forest cover that would provide similar vegetation densities to those of temperate and tropical areas such as South East Asia."[53]

Even though Canada didn't officially go into battle, thousands of Canadians served in the US military during the war. The Pearson government failed to prosecute Canadians for violating the Foreign Enlistment Act.[54]

Pearson even found little problem with the Johnson administration turning to South Korean mercenaries in 1965. Despite Defence Minister Paul Hellyer's desire to "consider what action might be taken to prevent it", the prime minister thought "it would not be a wise course for Canada to interfere".[55] Apparently, the South Korean mercenaries had a policy of killing one in 10 civilians in the villages they occupied. According to one study, they were responsible for at least a dozen massacres of a hundred or more people and dozens where 20 or more were killed.[56]

As part of the International Control Commission (ICC) for Vietnam, Ottawa played an important role in supporting US aggression. As noted previously, Canada represented the West, Poland the Eastern bloc and India was the neutral member. The ICC was supposed to enforce the implementation of the Geneva Accords and the peaceful reunification of Vietnam. Instead, Canada's representatives helped blunt ICC condemnation of Washington's bombing of North Vietnam and troop buildup in the South (under the Geneva Accords the US was allowed 685 military advisors).[57] *Partner to Behemoth* describes Ottawa's unwavering support for US policy at the ICC: "The most dramatic illustration of this was the minority report of the Canadian delegation on the ICC on February 13, 1965. The majority report by India and Poland condemned the beginning of American bombings of North Vietnam. Canadian dissent made no mention of the bombings and stated that 'continuing instability' in Vietnam was the result of 'the deliberate and persistent pursuit of aggressive but largely covert policies by North Vietnam directed against South Vietnam.' The Canadian position was almost a carbon copy of the quickly discredited US State Department White paper, Aggression from the North."[58]

Pearson's statements in the House reflected this position. Asked about the Geneva Accords in February 1965 he said: "If that settlement has not worked out satisfactorily — and it has not — the major share of responsibility must be directed toward the government of North Vietnam and those who have supported it. They have not lived up to that agreement from the beginning and have done their best to make it unworkable."

Canadian soldiers and diplomats on the ICC acted as US spies. Brigadier Donald Ketcheson admitted that he "regularly furnished the CIA with information about [North Vietnamese] troop movements."[59] External Affairs was "unofficially" aware, but "looked the other way."[60] A Canadian physician and former External Aid Office (precursor to CIDA) worker explained "back in the summer of 1965 we would give the Americans any tidbits we picked up — anything we thought of importance to the Americans we would tell them. When the Americans bombed oil storage tanks outside Hanoi, we had a delegation in Hanoi and took a number of pictures on the ground of oil tanks being blasted by American planes."[61]

According to *Quiet Complicity*, "Washington regarded [Canada's ICC Commissioner Blair] Seaborne as its eyes, ears and mouth in Hanoi. ... He was instructed to bring back political intelligence on the level of war weariness among the North Vietnamese, on the state of their economy, on the respective influence of the Russians and the Chinese and on possible divisions among the leaders."[62]

Most shockingly, Seaborne delivered US bombing threats to the North on a number of occasions in 1964. Prior to the wide-scale US bombing Seaborne received "instructions" from Washington to convey a carrot and- stick policy to the North Vietnamese.[63] On one occasion he told officials in Hanoi "US public and official patience with North Vietnamese aggression is growing extremely thin" and "if the DRV [North Vietnam] persists in its present course, it can expect to suffer the consequences."[64] According to the *Pentagon Papers* — leaked internal government documents — Pearson okayed Seaborne's actions. The *Pentagon Papers* describe a May 28, 1964 meeting the Prime Minister had with Lyndon Johnson at a New York hotel: "Pearson after expressing willingness to lend Canadian good offices to this endeavor, indicated some concern about this (sic) nature of the 'sticks'. He stipulated that he would have great reservations about the use of nuclear weapons, but indicated that the punitive striking of discriminate targets by careful iron bomb attacks would be 'a different thing'. He said he would personally understand our resort to such measures if the messages transmitted through the Canadian channel failed to produce any alleviation of North Vietnamese aggression, and that Canada would transmit messages around this framework."[65] A leading foreign policy advisor to Presidents Kennedy and Johnston, William P. Bundy, confirmed the *Pentagon Papers* account. "Beginning as early as June 1964 Pearson had, as far as I could tell, willingly and fully cooperated in having Seaborne convey those messages that were combination of a carrot and stick."[66]

In so doing the Nobel laureate enabled a serious war crime. "By allowing Seaborne to carry U.S. ultimatums to Hanoi", *Snow Job* concludes, "the [Pearson] government accepted an active role in the unfolding of this [US] escalation scenario. Once the bombings had begun, Ottawa tried to excuse them by again harping on North Vietnam's aggression in the South."[67]

The US "saturation" bombing of the North lasted for three and a half years. Air Force Chief of Staff, Curtis LeMay, explained: "They've got to draw in their horns and stop their aggression, or we're going to bomb them back into the Stone Age."[68] All types of infrastructure were targeted, including hospitals, bridges, roads etc. A September 1967 *Christian Science Monitor* article noted: "Dikes in the fertile Red River delta — North Vietnam's rice basket — have come under increasing air attack lately. The American

Lester Pearson's Peacekeeping

bombing appears intended not only to demoralize and harass the population in the most densely populated region of the country, but also to destroy the rice crops in the vast alluvial plains with their vulnerable open spaces ... here in the delta region, whose paddy fields provide the bulk of the rice supply of 17 million North Vietnamese, there have been almost daily attacks on dikes along the numerous small confluences of the Red River. ... The pattern of the bombing in the delta seems evident — to interdict agricultural production. No military targets are visible in the dikes. The heaviest artillery pieces we saw were antiquated rifles of the peasant militia."[69]

Upwards of a hundred thousand North Vietnamese were killed in bombing raids and large swaths of the North were destroyed. Pearson clearly abetted this flagrant war crime. For this reason alone he may be better described as a war criminal than a great Canadian. His support for the overthrow of the Indonesian government and the massacre of hundreds of thousands in that country is further evidence of Pearson's flagrant disregard for the rights of civilian populations.

Again, it is up to the reader as truth and reconciliation commissioner to decide the truth about Mike Pearson.

8. Conclusion — Leading by Deferring to Power

Lester Pearson clearly failed to live up to the Preamble of the United Nations Charter. He repeatedly supported the most powerful countries' use of force to get their way. He did little to stop and sometimes defended gross human rights violations in countries such as South Africa and Brazil. He consistently sided with the rich and powerful over improved rights and social conditions for the majority of the world. Mike Pearson's Canada was not a good neighbour to those struggling to overcome colonialism.

Two questions immediately arise: What was Pearson's motivation? And, what is it about his legacy that keeps his name alive in current Canadian foreign policy debates?

To answer the first question, there is nothing to suggest that Pearson wanted Canadian troops to kill Koreans or the US to destroy Vietnam. Or that he was any more racist than the average Canadian. By all accounts, he was a congenial fellow who loved his children. So why did he contribute to so much violence and injustice?

Pearson's overriding motivation was to advance his career, which isn't to say that he didn't believe in much of what he did. Reared on the White Man's Burden and other ideas justifying British imperialism, it was relatively easy for Pearson to support the US-directed equivalent.

Though Pearson may have generally aligned his worldview with the policies he pursued, the esteemed diplomat espoused contradictory ideas and backed decisions not to his liking. When he disagreed with policy favoured by powerful forces, ambition usually sharpened his thinking. Political colleague Jean Marchand called Pearson "a man of principle", but "he thought that all principles were quite flexible."[1] Pearson had a talent for gauging the interests of the powerful and shifting his position accordingly. Long-time External Affairs colleague Escott Reid wrote in his diary: "I now realize better Mike's ability to rise in favour. He is agile at quitting a position when he finds that the powers don't like it."[2]

Highly charismatic in small groups, Pearson's social skills allowed him to befriend influential individuals. *Lester Pearson: Diplomat and Politician* explains: "During his period in Washington, Pearson became one of the most popular foreign diplomats with American government officials and journalists alike. He made close friends in both circles."[3] As a general rule, Pearson sought out those who might be climbing the ranks. According to one biography, for instance, when dispatched to the US capital Pearson "identified [future Secretary of State Dean] Acheson early as a comer in Washington and courted him."[4]

Throughout his career Pearson deferred to power, even when this contributed to grave injustice. It's called realism in international relations theory. Prominent right-wing military historian Sean Maloney aptly dubbed the Nobel laureate "an astute realist".[5]

When Pearson pushed humanistic policies his decision was usually motivated by power politics, not compassion. The peacekeeping mission in Egypt, criticism of Soviet aggression in Eastern Europe and the Colombo Plan aid program are examples. Similarly, he distanced Canada (slightly) from the white supremacist regimes in southern Africa because of African and Asian countries pressure, not out of moral indignation.[6]

An effective realist makes decisions based on the international balance of power or other tactical considerations and then cites a humanitarian motive to convince the general public. In a biography of his External Affairs colleague, John Holmes, Royal Military College professor Adam Chapnick points out that Pearson believed "idealism certainly had a place, its main role was in promoting government policy at home, not in shaping strategic thinking."[7]

Due to his role in peacekeeping Pearson is associated with multilateralism, particularly the UN. He wholeheartedly backed the international institutions created after World War II (NATO, IMF/World Bank and UN), which largely advanced the Washington-led world order. (For its first two decades the UN was little more than an arm of the State Department.) It is fair to say that Pearson preferred to see US power projected through the UN, NATO or other multilateral forums. Pearson was not ideological, however. He also supported unilateral American interventions in Vietnam, Guatemala and the Dominican Republic. Some argue that Pearson supported NATO or the UN because Canada was less likely to be overwhelmed by Washington in a multilateral forum than in bilateral negotiations. In a discussion of Pearson's foreign policy Linda McQaig quotes a military strategist who says "the appeal of NATO in Ottawa was that it was seen as 'an offset to excessive American influence.'"[8] It may be true that bilateral negotiations with Washington could feel overwhelming to Canadian officials, but this implies that Ottawa decision-makers opposed US policy towards the rest of the world. This is nonsense. Occasionally Ottawa disagreed with US tactics or was unwilling to devote the resources requested to support a particular US-led action but the Canadian elite rarely disagreed with the substance of US foreign policy.

Rather than a means to protect humanistic Canadian decision-makers from aggressive American foreign policy, multilateral endeavors strengthened the western alliance all the while garnering greater domestic and Third World legitimacy, even when US-led. The CCF/NDP regularly called for greater UN involvement in foreign affairs. Pearson understood that newly independent countries were more likely to support (or at least less likely to criticize) UN-approved missions. Partly to gain Indian support, for instance, he pushed to expand the UN's role in the US-initiated Korean War.

The Commonwealth was another multilateral forum that Canada's famed statesmen supported. Early Canadian aid was made available to countries that joined the Commonwealth, an organization rooted in British imperialism. Washington generally approved. The important US planning document NSC 68 explained that "a strengthening of the British position is needed if the stability of the Commonwealth is not to be impaired and if it is to be a focus of resistance to Communist expansion in South and South-East Asia."[9]

The military alliance of leading capitalist nations, NATO, was Mike's primary multilateral concern. In 1963 he told Parliament: "NATO has been the foundation of the foreign policy of Canadian governments ever since it was formed in 1949, and it will continue to be so."[10]

Only exaggerating slightly, Pierre Trudeau claimed that during the Pearson years "we had no defence policy, so to speak, except that of NATO. And our defence policy had determined all of our foreign-policy. And we had no foreign policy of any importance except that which flowed from NATO."[11] When Trudeau became prime minister in 1968 he initiated a review of Canadian foreign policy that questioned Canada's participation in NATO. Horrified, Pearson immediately asked to discuss the issue with Trudeau and External Affairs Minister Mitchell Sharp.[12] Apparently, this was the only time he got involved in government business after retiring.

At the end of his career Pearson described the "formation of NATO", not peacekeeping, as the "most important thing I participated in."[13] This may surprise those who associate him with peacekeeping but it is consistent with his objective during the Suez Crisis. Pearson pushed to resolve the conflict in Egypt largely to save NATO from internal division. The Suez Crisis demonstrates how disunity — it's known as a "crisis" because Washington opposed the British/French/Israeli invasion — weakened the West. This division benefited nationalist Egyptian President Nasser and the former colonies gathered together in the Non-Aligned Movement.

NATO was created precisely to avoid such a fracturing among the leading capitalist countries. Pearson described it to the House in 1953 as "the unity and strength that have been so patiently and effectively built up, especially since the establishment of NATO."[14] In effect, the north Atlantic alliance was designed to maintain unity among the historic colonial powers — and the US — in the midst of a de-colonizing world.

Lester Pearson's Peacekeeping

In the annals of Canadian foreign policy, Suez represents Ottawa's decisive break from London. While McQuaig may believe that Pearson "managed to create a role for Canada outside the U.S. sphere of influence," in fact he was the individual most responsible for Canada's post-World War II shift away from British imperialism and towards the US version.[15] In 1941 Pearson described his thinking: "It is inevitable that, as a North American country, Canada should develop North American points of view."[16] In his *Memoirs* Pearson further explained: "My experience in Washington [between 1942 and 1946] convinced me that relations with our neighbour were bound to be far and away the most important part of Canada's foreign-policy."[17] As a result, Pearson was terribly disappointed when Mackenzie King stopped secret free trade negotiations with the US in the spring of 1948.[18]

Sometimes Pearson was astoundingly forthright about his vision of Canada-US relations. He believed this country "voluntarily and wholeheartedly accepted the leadership of the United States" and even argued that Canada had a special role "interpreting US foreign policy to other nations."[19]

For his steadfast support of the Washington-led world order Pearson was praised by the dominant North American media and won the Nobel Peace Prize. More significantly, he became the only Canadian politician ever featured on a US bubblegum card.[20]

Earlier than many other decision-makers, Mike recognized that an expanded US sphere of influence would be a boon to the Canadian elite (and without formal colonies Ottawa had little reason to fear US encroachment in the Global South). No country was better placed to benefit from growing US hegemony. Here's a small sample of the close ties between the Canadian and American elite during this period: Canada's longest serving prime minister, Mackenzie

Lester Pearson's Peacekeeping

King, worked for the influential Rockefeller family; Pearson's uncle was an executive in the Chicago-based meat packing company made infamous in Upton Sinclair's novel *The Jungle*; the mother of long-time Secretary of State, Dean Acheson, was from a wealthy Canadian family; Oshawa, Ontario's Samuel McLaughlin was vice-president, long-time board member and leading shareholder of General Motors, the US's largest corporation.

A few years after Pearson retired, Wallace Clement investigated the ties between the Canadian and US business class. He found extensive interlocking directorships (business executives sitting on each other's corporate boards). *Continental Corporate Power* explains: "Overall, 63 of the 113 dominant corporations in Canada (or 56%) are interlocked with US dominants; 73 of the 194 dominant corporations in the United States have interlocks with Canadian dominants. ... direct interlocks are signs of strength, both those from US dominants to independent Canadian dominants, which reflect the ability of the Canadian elite to attract important members of the US elite, and those from independent Canadian dominants to US dominants, which reflect a desire by members of the US elite to attract members of the indigenous Canadian elite."[21]

Canadian corporations often benefited directly from US imperialism. With US national banks not allowed to establish foreign branches until 1914, Canadian banks acted for the US government after Washington took control of Cuba and the Philippines following the 1898-1902 Spanish-American war. When Pearson was prime minister, Falconbridge benefited from the US invasion of the Dominican Republic and Brascan profited from Washington's role in ousting Joao Goulart in Brazil (a year after the coup USAID even gave the Canadian company a $40 million loan for its operations in Brazil).[22]

Lester Pearson's Peacekeeping

This book focuses on Canada's most influential post World War II international-affairs decision maker. But, one individual does not make a country's foreign policy. To a large degree, Pearson pursued policies similar to those of his predecessor and successor. On some issues the Trudeau government was slightly more independent and even humane, notably on Palestine and Cuba. For his part, Diefenbaker was less interested in deepening relations with the US military. Nonetheless, there's much more continuity than difference between various Canadian governments' foreign policies.

As prime minister, minister for external affairs and External Affairs official, Pearson represented an entire power structure. His decisions were influenced by prevailing Christian, patriarchal and euro-centric ideologies. Early in his career Pearson referred to the "Anglo-Saxon peoples" and in a 1951 report he described "the protection of our heritage of Christian civilization" as an "aspect of our external affairs."[23]

The country Pearson represented on the international stage was built by dispossessing its First Peoples. Not until after Pearson's time as foreign minister were Status Indians able to vote and it was only three years into his term that the Indian Act was amended, allowing First Nations to practice their religious/cultural ceremonies (such as potlatches, pow-wows, sweat lodges and sun dances). In short, the state Pearson represented internationally was a successful colonial enterprise. On at least one occasion he explicitly equated foreign policy with the subjugation of First Nations. In an April 1951 speech to the Canadian Club about Korea and the Cold War Pearson said: "We are faced now with a situation similar in some respects to that which confronted our fore-fathers in early colonial days when they plowed the land with a rifle slung on the shoulder. If they stuck to the plow and left the rifle at home, they would have been easy victims for any savages lurking in the woods."[24]

To a large extent the class nature of Canadian society determined foreign-policy decision-making. Though not wealthy himself, Pearson had a privileged upbringing and enjoyed the company of the financial elite. "He was most comfortable in common rooms, millionaire's villas, and London men's clubs", noted *The Worldly Years*.[25] Pearson vacationed at the Rockefeller family estate in the Caribbean and in 1947 he turned down a lucrative offer to become president of the Rockefeller Foundation.[26] To supplement Pearson's salary some of his wealthy friends created a trust fund known as the Algoma Fishing and Conservation Society.[27] Leading Canadian capitalist Walter Gordon, notes his biography, raised "more than $100,000 [$850,000 in today's money] from his wealthy friends for a trust fund that would ensure that the Pearsons would not suffer from the uncertainties of public life."[28] The fund paid $400 a month (about $3,500 today).[29]

Presumably, those who donated to the Algoma Fishing and Conservation Society had stocks in Canadian companies invested around the world. During Pearson's career Canadian banks dominated the Caribbean financial sector while the Aluminum Company of Canada (Alcan) was a major player in Jamaica and the Cuban-Canadian sugar company owned a great deal of territory in that country. Brascan was one of the biggest companies in Latin America while Toronto-based Bata was the world's largest shoemaker. To a large extent the owners and executives of these internationally focused businesses shaped Canada's global affairs.

The back-and-forth between corporate boardrooms and public office strengthened business influence over international policy. As noted above long-time Liberal civil servant, Mitchell Sharp left his position as deputy minister in the Department of Trade and Commerce to become vice-president of Brascan (known as the "Canadian Octopus" in Brazil). Prime Minister Pearson lured Sharp back to politics, appointing him minister of finance. Similarly, Pearson's minister of trade and commerce, Robert Winters, left politics in 1968 to become president of Brascan.

The rich also influenced foreign-policy debates through their ownership of the media. A special March 1969 Senate committee investigating media concentration found that Canadian "information" services were dominated by "an extremely privileged group of businessmen."[30] Three newspaper chains — Southam, Financial Post Publications and Thomson Newspapers — controlled nearly half of English Canada's daily newspapers.[31] Owners unsatisfied with international coverage could remove the paper's editor. *Time* magazine described an example of this at the Southam-owned *Ottawa Citizen* in the spring of 1955. "When [editor Charles James] Woodsworth came out against the rearmament of West Germany, publisher [Robert] Southam got fed up.... [and] quietly sacked his editor."[32]

Beyond the media, moneyed interests shaped the discussion of international affairs by financing private endeavors. In December 1941, for instance, the Rockefeller Foundation renewed a $20,000 (about $300,000 today) grant for the Canadian Institute for International Affairs (CIIA), the leading non-governmental foreign policy focused organization. The money covered more than half of the CIIA's yearly budget (Pearson was close to long-time CIIA head John Holmes).[33] In another example, the Donner family directly influenced coverage of Pearson's legacy. The Donner Foundation put up $15,000 ($90,000 today) to hire writing help for Pearson's one thousand page *Memoirs*, which was completed after his death.[34]

Ultimately, it was a relatively small number of businesspeople, intellectuals and politicians who shaped foreign policy. As a result, External Affairs was the "least partisan of portfolios", noted one Pearson biography.[35] Minister Pearson explained: "I am fortunate also in the fact that the external policy of Canada, in its principles and objectives, to the extent any policy can be in a Parliamentary system of government is nonpartisan in character; and of course I'm beneficiary of that happy circumstance. I think it makes my job, at least so far as Parliament is concerned, much easier than that of my colleagues."[36]

The Korean War was supported across party lines. *Strange Battleground* notes: "All parties in the House were in agreement that Canada should do something and that quickly; all agreed to support the government in whatever action it deemed necessary to demonstrate the effectiveness of collective security."[37] Similarly, on atomic weapons — among the most important issues of the day — Pearson had a great deal of room to maneuver. *Pearson and Canada's Role in Nuclear Disarmament and Arms Control Negotiations, 1945-1957* explains: "The government could truthfully claim that the opposition parties supported its policy. It was virtually given a blank cheque to make policy on the military aspects of atomic energy for the next decade."[38] Pearson obviously preferred it this way. As a civil servant he pushed for bureaucratic control over foreign policy. When he was undersecretary of External Affairs (its highest non-political position) Pearson argued that cabinet shouldn't discuss international affairs more than necessary.[39] He also thought unelected civil servants should play a greater role in international forums. "There are times when I think we might be well advised to leave more of it to the diplomats. They are trained for the job and they are usually happy to conduct a negotiation without issuing a progress report after each 20 minutes."[40]

Pearson believed professionals should direct foreign policy and he didn't appreciate it when other governments tried to convince ordinary Canadians of their position. In January 1954 he criticized Moscow for their "incessant and direct appeal to peoples over the heads of governments."[41]

Popular participation in shaping foreign policy was unnecessary since all Canadians had common international interests. Pearson explained: "I believe also that Canada's external affairs should, to the greatest possible extent, though always subject to the legitimate requirements of responsible Parliamentary government, be kept on a non-partisan basis. After all, we are all Canadians, or should be, before we are Liberals, Conservatives or CCFers [NDPers], and before we are Quebéckers or Manitobans."[42] Are we really to believe that the CEO of Canada's largest multinational firm has the same foreign-policy interests as a longshoreman?

If Pearson's foreign policy was to be summarized the best words to describe it would be violent or unjust not peaceful or internationalist. Put plainly, the historical record has been stood on its head. For most of the intelligentsia and Canadian population Pearson has become little more than a mythical construct divorced from the man's record. Unfortunately, some progressives are willing to fit anything into their preconceived notions, however damaging it may be. For example, in an attempt to square his admiration of NATO with her desire to portray Pearson as a peace promoting, anti-American internationalist Linda McQuaig claims the north Atlantic alliance challenged Washington. "There were even fears at the outset that Washington would retreat back into isolationism and decline to participate... In supporting NATO, Canada [Pearson] was also promoting an internationalist vision of collective security, rather than simply tying itself and its security to Washington."[43] Implying that NATO was not part of expanding the US centered imperial order distorts 60 years of Canadian foreign policy. By understanding Pearson's motivation in NATO's creation we can better make sense of the organization's recent role in Afghanistan, Libya and the former Yugoslavia.

It makes sense for someone who believes in Western power and an elite-dominated foreign policy to portray Pearson positively. But why would someone on the Left deify him? This brings us back to the second question asked at the beginning of this chapter: What is it about his legacy that keeps his name alive in current Canadian foreign policy debates?

The best explanation is also the simplest. Pearson got good press. He is by far Canada's best-known international statesman. He set the standard by which ambitious foreign policy practitioners will be judged. If diplomatic fame and official glory are your goals, it helps to follow in his footsteps, or at least to claim Mike would be on your side in any current debate.

For example, some commentators argue persuasively that Pearson would have promoted the Responsibility to Protect (R2P) if he were in office today. R2P asserts that where gross human rights abuses occur it is the duty of the international community to intervene, over and above considerations of state sovereignty. "The principle of non-intervention yields to the international responsibility to protect."[44] On paper this Canadian-promoted doctrine is a good idea, unless one considers national borders, usually created through colonial violence, sacrosanct. But who decides when gross human rights abuses are occurring? Was the US responsible for gross human rights abuses in Iraq? Even though credible reports found that the 2003 US invasion and subsequent occupation led to hundreds of thousands of Iraqi deaths, leading R2P proponents never called on the international community to intervene in Washington.[45]

Rather than a tool to improve international human rights standards, R2P has been used by the powerful against the weak. Many liberal commentators/ex-politicians invoked R2P to justify NATO's 2011 bombing of Libya. During that war Canadian-commanded NATO fighter jets dropped thousands of bombs in a bid to secure regime change in the oil-rich nation. In the early 2000s Liberal government officials cited R2P to cut off assistance to Haiti's elected government and to invade that country.[46] Thousands were killed after the US/France/Canada intervention and a highly impoverished society became even poorer.[47] R2P further undermines state sovereignty, which provides the weakest states with some protection from the most powerful. This is the main reason why Latin American, Asian and African countries have largely opposed attempts to incorporate R2P into international law.

For these reasons Pearson may well have been a proponent of R2P if he were alive today. Mike would likely have appreciated the fact that R2P can be used as an ideological mask to justify imperial interventions. More sophisticated in their marketing, those backing R2P pursue international policies not substantially different from Stephen Harper or George W. Bush's neo-conservatives. As is the case with high profile proponents of R2P (such as former Liberal leader Michael Ignatieff and Foreign Affairs Minister Lloyd Axworthy), Pearson talked about peace and justice while pursuing an aggressive policy. He pushed to send troops to Korea and backed the US destruction of Vietnam but after leaving office he wrote a book called *Peace in Family of Man*. He even put an antiwar gloss on his move to acquire nuclear tipped Bomarc missiles in 1963. "By concentrating our emotions on a particular kind of weapon," the Prime Minister exalted, "we are in danger of obscuring the real issue, which is disarmament and outlawing war as an instrument of national policy."[48] Pearson made that statement as he enabled Washington to escalate its war on Vietnam. In other words, Pearson was brilliant at obfuscation, and even lying, to cover the reality of his actual foreign policy. This seems to be a skill much admired in certain diplomatic circles.

The other part of the answer to why Pearson's international legacy continues to be upheld is the limited range of debate regarding foreign policy. It is nearly impossible to survive as a mainstream commentator/politician if you say Canadian foreign policy has always been self-serving/elite-driven or that no government has come even close to reflecting their self-professed ideals on the international stage. Rather than forthrightly criticize this country's history, most critical commentators oppose current policy by calling for a return to a mythical 'golden era' of Canadian foreign policy. This type of criticism is more acceptable, partly because linking criticism of ongoing practices to a 'golden era' of progressive Canadian foreign policy one (implicitly) downplays the structural character of the problem.

Since only a narrow spectrum of opinion is permitted in the dominant media, debates about foreign affairs are deeply flawed. Almost all mainstream commentators express trust in western interventions. Most of those who are given a position to comment support Western imperialism, either the hardline neoconservative version or a softer Responsibility to Protect/

peacekeeping form. Almost no one says the Global South would do better with less Canada.

In a February 2008 *National Post* commentary right-wing historian Jack Granatstein argued that on foreign policy Stephen Harper is Lester Pearson's heir. Yes and no. As I've noted elsewhere, Harper militarized foreign policy, supported Israeli crimes, undermined Latin American democracy and weakened important international agreements. Nonetheless, Pearson was culpable for more death and destruction. The counterinsurgency war in Afghanistan and bombing of Libya do not compare with the killing fields in Korea where as many as four million people died. And Pearson threatened to resign if Canada failed to send ground troops.

It is not that Harper is nicer, but rather the world is a little better. Direct colonialism and open racism are no longer commonplace. Additionally, average Canadians are more engaged in international affairs than during Pearson's time in office. In an unprecedented move, the anti-war movement stopped Jean Chretien's Liberal government from officially endorsing the Bush administration's "coalition of the willing", which invaded Iraq (Ottawa did, however, provide various other forms of support). Hundreds of thousands protested before the war even began.

Support for Palestinian rights may provide the clearest example of the growth in popular consciousness. In 1947 Pearson played a major part in the diplomatic moves that enabled the destruction of Palestinian society, the "nakba". Yet few Canadians protested Canada's complicity in this injustice. In contrast, when Israeli forces killed 1,400 Palestinians in Gaza at the end of 2008/ early 2009, tens of thousands demonstrated against the bombing and Harper's complicity therein. (Interestingly, Harper left it to

Foreign Affairs Minister Lawrence Cannon to publicly justify Israel's 22-day assault against Gaza. Reportedly, Harper was wary of the bad publicity he received for calling Israel's 33-day attack on Lebanon in 2006 a "measured response" to Hezbollah incursions). Though still unable to determine policy, the pro-Palestinian movement in Canada is infinitely stronger today.

The greater internationalism that exists today is why more Canadians consider Harper's foreign policy destructive. It's rare for someone who doesn't know/care about the rest of the world to oppose their government's foreign policy.

Unfortunately, the social relations that shaped Pearson's foreign policy continue to varying degrees. Though there have been improvements, there is a long way to go in building a proper sense of international solidarity. Partly because of this, Canadian foreign affairs is still dominated by a small elite with most of the population shut out of the discussion. Another reason the elite dominate foreign policy is the highly unequal distribution of resources in our society, which has become even more extreme since Pearson was in office.

Only when large numbers of ordinary citizens take Canada's role in the world seriously will an independent and justice-enriching foreign policy be possible. Readers of this book have been asked to think of themselves as members of a truth and reconciliation commission looking into Canada's foreign policy past. Perhaps such a citizens commission needs to be set up. Honest Canadians need to confront the truth of what has been done in our name. Mythologizing this country's foreign policy past does not help people in understanding our current reality. The truth may hurt, but it also sets you free.

Bibliography

Abella Irving & Harold Martin Troper, None is Too Many: Canada and the Jews of Europe, 1933-1948. Lester & Orpen Dennys, 1982

Andrew Arthur, The Rise and Fall of a Middle Power: Canadian Diplomacy from King to Mulroney. Lorimer, 1993

Arruda Marcos & de Souza Herbert & Afonso Carlos, The Multinational Corporations and Brazil: the Impact of Multinational Corporations in the Contemporary Brazilian Economy. Brazilian Studies, Latin America Research Unit, 1975

Austin Alvyn, Saving China: Canadian Missionaries in the Middle Kingdom, 1888-1959. University of Toronto Press, 1986

Azzi Stephen, Walter Gordon and the Rise of Canadian Nationalism. McGill-Queen's University Press, 1999

Balawyder Aloysius, In the Clutches of the Kremlin: Canadian-East European Relations (1945-1962). East European Monographs Columbia University Press, 2000

Balawyder Aloysius, On the Road to Freedom: Canadian-East European Relations, 1963-1991. East European Monographs Columbia University Press, 2005

Barbosa Rosana, Brazil and Canada in the Americas. Gorsebrook Research Institute, 2007

Beal John Robinson, Pearson of Canada. Sloan and Pearce, 1964

Bercuson David J, Canada and the Birth of Israel: A Study in Canadian Foreign Policy. University of Toronto Press, 1985

Bercuson David J, Blood on the Hills: the Canadian Army in the Korean War. University of Toronto Press, 1999

Bercuson David J, True Patriot: the Life of Brooke Claxton, 1898-1960. University of Toronto Press, 1993

Blanchette Arthur E, Canadian Foreign Policy, 1945-2000: Major Documents and Speeches. Golden Dog Press, 2000

Blum William, Killing Hope: U.S. Military and CIA interventions Since World War II. Common Courage Press, 2004

Bothwell Robert, Pearson His Life and World. McGraw-Hill Ryerson, 1978

Bothwell Robert, Alliance and Illusion: Canada and the World, 1945-1984. UBC Press, 2007

Bristman Barry, In the Strategic Interests of Canada: Canadian Arms Sales to Israel and Other Middle East States, 1949-1956. MA thesis, University of Calgary, 1992

Buckley Brian, Canada's Early Nuclear policy: Fate, Chance, and Character. McGill-Queen's University Press, 2000

Cardwell Curt, NSC 68 and the Political Economy of the Early Cold War. Cambridge University Press, 2011

Carroll Michael K, Pearson's Peacekeepers: Canada and the United Nations Emergency Force, 1956-67. UBC Press, 2009

Carty Robert & Virginia Smith & Latin American Working Group, Perpetuating Poverty: the Political Economy of Canadian Foreign Aid. Between the Lines, 1981

Chapnick Adam, The Middle Power Project: Canada and the Founding of the United Nations. UBC Press, 2005

Chapnick Adam, Canada's Voice: the Public Life of John Wendell Holmes. UBC Press, 2009

Chodos Robert & Murphy Rae, Let Us Prey. Lorimer, 1974

Chomsky Noam, What Uncle Sam Really Wants. Odonian Press, 1992

Chomsky Noam, Year 501: the Conquest Continues. Black Rose Books, 1993

Chomsky Noam, At War With Asia. Pantheon Books 1970

Chomsky Noam & Edward Herman. The Washington Connection and Third World Fascism. South End, 1979

Chomsky Noam, American Power and the New Mandarins. Pantheon Books, 1969

Chomsky Noam & Mitchell Peter R & Schoeffel John, Understanding Power. New Press, 2002

Clearwater John, Canadian Nuclear Weapons: the Untold Story of Canada's Cold War Arsenal. Dundurn Press, 1998

Clearwater John, "Just dummies": Cruise Missile Testing in Canada. University of Calgary Press, 2006

Clement Wallace, Continental Corporate Power. McClelland and Stewart, 1977

Cohen Andrew, Lester B. Pearson. Penguin, 2008

Delvoie Louis A, Canada and Egypt: From Antagonism to Partnership. Centre for International Relations Queen's University, 1997

Dewitt David Brian & Kirton John J. Canada as a Principal Power: a Study in Foreign Policy and International Relations. Wiley, 1983

Eayrs James George, Northern Approaches: Canada and the Search for Peace. Macmillan, 1961

Eayrs James George, The Commonwealth and Suez; a Documentary Survey. Oxford University Press, 1964

English John, Shadow of Heaven: the Life of Lester Pearson. Lester & Orpen Dennys, 1992

English John, The Worldly Years: the Life of Lester Pearson. Vintage Books, 1993

Evans Paul M & Frolic Michael B, Reluctant Adversaries: Canada and the People's Republic of China, 1949-1970. University of Toronto Press, 1991

Finch Ron, Exporting Danger: a History of the Canadian Nuclear Energy Export Programme. Black Rose Books, 1986

Finkelstein Norman G, Image and Reality of the Israel-Palestine Conflict. Verso, 2003

Freeman Linda, The Ambiguous Champion: Canada and South Africa in the Trudeau and Mulroney Years. University of Toronto Press, 1997

Gaffen Fred, Unknown Warriors: Canadians in Vietnam. Dundurn Press, 1990

Ganser Daniele, NATO's Secret Armies: Operation GLADIO and Terrorism in Western Europe. Routledge, 2005

Gendron Robin Stewart Towards a Francophone Community: Canada's Relations with France and French Africa, 1945-1968. McGill-Queen's University Press, 2006.

Gimblett Richard Howard & Haydon Peter T & Griffiths Ann L, Canadian Gunboat Diplomacy: the Canadian Navy and Foreign Policy. Centre for Foreign Policy Studies, 2000

Gordon Neve, Israel's Occupation. University of California Press, 2008

Harbottle Michael, The Blue Berets. Stackpole Books, 1972

Hart-Landsberg Martin, Korea: Division, Reunification, and U.S. Foreign Policy. Monthly Review Press, 1998

Haydon Peter Trevor, The 1962 Cuban Missile Crisis: Canadian Involvement Reconsidered. Canadian Institute of Strategic Studies, 1993

Heinbecker Paul & Momani Bessma Canada and the Middle East: In Theory and Practice. Wilfrid Laurier University Press (CIGI), 2007

Hilal Ali al-Din, Canadian Foreign Policy and the Palestine Problem. Middle East Research Centre Ottawa, 1970

Hillmer Norman, Pearson: Unlikely Gladiator. McGill-Queen's University Press, 1999

Howell Thomas A & Rajasooria Jeffrey P, Ghana and Nkrumah. Facts on File, 1972

Holmes John Wendell, The Shaping of Peace: Canada and the Search for World Order, Vol 2. University of Toronto Press, 1979

Hull William L, The Fall and Rise of Israel: the Story of the Jewish People During the Time of Their Dispersal and Regathering. Zondervan, 1954

Ismael Tareq Y, Canadian Arab Relations: Policy and Perspectives. Jerusalem International Pub. House, 1984

Jervis Robert, The Meaning of the Nuclear Revolution: Statecraft and the Prospect of Armageddon. Cornell University Press, 1989

Kaplan William, Canadian Maverick: the Life and Times of Ivan C. Rand. University of Toronto Press, 2009

Kay Zachariah, Canada and Palestine: The Politics of Non-Commitment. Israel University Press, 1978

Kay Zachariah, The Diplomacy of Impartiality: Canada and Israel, 1958-1968. Wilfred Laurier University Press, 2010

Khalidi Rashid, The Iron Cage: the Story of the Palestinian Struggle for Statehood. Beacon Press, 2006

Kinzer Stephen, All the Shah's Men: an American Coup and the Roots of Middle East Terror. Wiley & Sons, 2003

Kirk John M & McKenna Peter, Canada-Cuba Relations: the Other Good Neighbor Policy. University Press of Florida, 1997

Lee Steven Hugh, Outposts of Empire: Korea, Vietnam and the Origins of the Cold War in Asia, 1949-1954. McGill-Queen's University Press, 1995

Levant Victor, Quiet Complicity: Canadian Involvement in the Vietnam War. Between the Lines, 1986

Levitt Joseph, Pearson and Canada's Role in Nuclear Disarmament and Arms Control Negotiations 1945-1957. McGill-Queen's University Press, 1993

LeVos Ernest, The War for Men's Minds: the Canadian Perspective of Foreign Policy in Asia, 1945 — 1957. University of Alberta Press, 1991

Lyon Peyton & Ismael Tareq Y, Canada and the Third World. Macmillan of Canada, 1976

MacLaren Roy, Commissions High: Canada in London, 1870-1971. McGill-Queen's University Press, 2006

MacMillan Francine, Parties Long Estranged: Canada and Australia in the Twentieth Century. UBC Press, 2003

Madsen Chris, Another Kind of Justice: Canadian Military Law from Confederation to Somalia. UBC Press, 1999

Maloney Sean M, Canada and UN Peacekeeping: Cold War by Other Means, 1945-1970. Vanwell, 2002

McFarlane Peter, Northern Shadows: Canadians and Central America. Between the Lines, 1989

McKercher B J C & Aronsen Lawrence, The North Atlantic Triangle in a Changing World: Anglo-American-Canadian Relations, 1902-1956. University of Toronto Press, 1996

McQuaig Linda, Holding the Bully's Coat: Canada and the U.S. Empire. Doubleday Canada, 2007

Morris Benny, 1948: a History of the First Arab-Israeli war. Yale University Press, 2008

Morrison David R, Aid and Ebb Tide: a History of CIDA and Canadian Development Assistance. Wilfrid Laurier University Press, 1998

Munton Don & John J Kirton, Canadian Foreign Policy: Selected Cases. Prentice-Hall Canada, 1992

Nash Knowlton, Kennedy and Diefenbaker: Fear and Loathing Across the Undefended Border. McClelland & Stewart, 1990

Netherton Alexander, In/Security: Canada in the post-9/11 World. Centre for Canadian Studies Simon Fraser University, 2005

Nossal Kim Richard, Rain Dancing: Sanctions in Canadian and Australian Foreign Policy. University of Toronto Press, 1994

Norton Roy Brent, Domestic Determinants of Foreign Policy: Newly Immigrated Ethnic Communities and the Canadian Foreign Policy-Making Process, 1984-1993. UMI Dissertation Services, 1999

Pappe Ilan, The Ethnic Cleansing of Palestine. Oneworld, 2006

Pearson Geoffrey, Seize the Day: Lester B. Pearson and Crisis Diplomacy. Carleton University Press, 1993

Pearson Lester B, The Four Faces of Peace and the International Outlook. Mead, 1964

Pearson Lester B, Words and Occasions. University of Toronto Press, 1970

Pearson Lester B, The Memoirs of the Right Honourable Lester B. Pearson. University of Toronto Press, 1972

Peck James, Washington's China: The National Security World, the Cold War, and the Origins of Globalism. University of Massachusetts Press, 2006

Price John, Orienting Canada: Race, Empire, and the Transpacific. UBC Press, 2011

Price John & Roy Patricia & Donaghy Greg, Contradictory Impulses: Canada and Japan in the Twentieth Century. UBC Press, 2008

Reford Robert W, Canada and Three Crises. Canadian Institute of International Affairs, 1968

Reid Escott, Radical Mandarin: the Memoirs of Escott Reid. University of Toronto Press, 1989

Regehr Ernie, Making a Killing: Canada's Arms Industry. McClelland & Stewart, 1975

Regehr Ernie, Arms Canada: The Deadly Business of Military Exports. Lorimer, 1987

Rochlin James Francis, Discovering the Americas: The Evolution of Canadian Foreign Policy Towards Latin America. UBC Press, 1994

Rosner Gabriella, The United Nations Emergency Force. Columbia University Press, 1963

Said Edward W, The End of the Peace Process: Oslo and After. Pantheon Books, 2000

Schlegel John P, The Deceptive Ash: Bilingualism and Canadian Policy in Africa: 1957-1971. University Press of America, 1978

Schlesinger Stephen C & Kinzer Stephen, Bitter Fruit: the Untold Story of the American Coup in Guatemala. Doubleday, 1982

Seager Allen & Etherton Alexander N & Froschauer Karl, In/Security: Canada in the Post 9/11. World Center for Canadian Studies, Simon Fraser University, 2005

Shaw Jacqueline T, Grudging Gifts: Canada, the Colombo Plan and the Formation of an Aid Policy. M.A. Dissertation Research Paper Carleton University, 1993

Smith Denis, Diplomacy of Fear: Canada and the Cold War, 1941-1948. University of Toronto Press, 1988

Smillie Ian, The Land of Lost Content: A History of CUSO. Deneau, 1985

Stairs Denis, The diplomacy of Constraint: Canada, the Korean War, and the United States. University of Toronto Press, 1974

Stairs Denis & Canadian Defence and Foreign Affairs Institute, In The National Interest: Canadian Foreign Policy in an Insecure World. Canadian Defence and Foreign Affairs Institute, 2003

Starnes John, Closely Guarded: A Life in Canadian Security and Intelligence. University of Toronto Press, 1998

Stone I F, The Hidden History of the Korean War. Monthly Review Press 1969

Stursberg Peter, Lester Person and the American Dilemma. Doubleday Canada, 1980

Taras David & Goldberg David H, The Domestic Battleground: Canada and the Israeli Conflict. McGill-Queens University Press, 1989

Taylor Alastair MacDonald & Cox David & Granatstein J L, Peacekeeping: International Challenge and Canadian Response. Canadian Institute of International Affairs, 1968

Taylor Charles, Snow Job: Canada, the United States and Vietnam (1954 to 1973). Anansi, 1974

Taylor Scott & Nolan Brian, Tested Mettle: Canada's Peacekeepers at War. Esprit de Corps Books, 1998

Tauber Eliezer, Personal Policy Making Canada's Role in the Adoption of the Palestine Partition Resolution. Greenwood, 2002

Tennyson Brian Douglas, Canadian Relations with South Africa: A Diplomatic History. University Press of America, 1982

Thakur Ramesh Chandra, Peacekeeping in Vietnam. University of Alberta Press, 1984

Thordarson Bruce, Lester Pearson: Diplomat and Politician. Oxford University Press, 1974

Thomson Dale, Louis St. Laurent: Canadian. St. Martin's Press, 1968

Watson Brent Byron, Far Eastern Tour: The Canadian Infantry in Korea, 1950-1953. McGill-Queen's University Press, 2002

Warnock John, Partner to Behemoth: The Military Policy of a Satellite Canada. New Press, 1970

Webster David, Fire and the Full Moon: Canada and Indonesia in a Decolonizing World. UBC Press, 2009

Whitaker Reginald & Marcuse Gary, Cold War Canada: The Making of a National Insecurity State, 1945-1957. University of Toronto Press, 1994

Wood Herbert Fairlie & Canada. Dept. of National Defence, Strange Battleground: The Operations in Korea and Their Effects on the Defence Policy of Canada. R. Duhamel Queen's Printer, 1966

Words and Deeds: Canada, Portugal, and Africa. Toronto Committee for the Liberation of Southern Africa, 1976

Wright Robert A & Lana Wylie, Our Place in the Sun: Canada and Cuba in the Castro Era. University of Toronto Press, 2009

Zinn Howard, A People's History of the United States: 1492-Present. HarperCollins, 2003

Endnotes

Introduction
1. Stursberg, Lester Person and the American Dilemma, vi
2. http://embassymag.ca/page/view/chatter-9-2-2009
3. http://openParliament.ca/politicians/132/
4. http://rabble.ca/books/reviews/2009/07/cost-war
5. Flavouring the Election Race with Memories of Liberalism Oct 25 2000

Chapter 1
1. Stursberg, Lester Pearson and the American Dilemma, ix, xii
2. English, The Worldly Years, 40
3. English, Shadow of Heaven, 93
4. Hillmer, Pearson: Unlikely Gladiator, 52
5. MacLaren, Commissions High, 195
6. Pearson, Memoirs 2, 30
7. English, Shadow of Heaven, 98
8. Cohen, Lester B. Pearson, 61
9. Pearson, Memoirs, 122
10. Cohen, Lester B. Pearson, 61
11. Stursberg, Lester Person and the American Dilemma, 28
12. Pearson, Memoirs 1, 208
13. Stursberg, Lester Pearson and the American Dilemma, 47
14. Price, Orienting Canada, 103
15. Price, Orienting Canada, 104
16. Nash, Kennedy and Diefenbaker, 144
17. Price, Orienting Canada, 94
18. Chapnick, The Middle Power Project, 135
19. MacMillan, Parties long estranged, 253
20. MacMillan, parties long estranged, 252
21. Hillmer, Pearson: unlikely gladiator, 40
22. Chapnick, The Middle Power Project, 138
23. Chapnick, The Middle Power Project, 138
24. Chapnick, The Middle Power Project, 138
25. Canadian Foreign policy Vol 13 #1, 2006
26. Bothwell, Pearson his life and world, 32

Chapter 2
1. McQuaig, Holding the Bully's Coat, 149
2. Whitaker, Cold War Canada, 68; Pearson, Memoirs 1, 234
3. Smith, Diplomacy of Fear, 167
4. Azzi, Walter Gordon and the Rise of Canadian Nationalism, 34
5. Whitaker, Cold War Canada, 266
6. English, Shadow of heaven, 301
7. Hansard May 28 1954, 5190
8. Hansard Jan 14 1957, 175
9. Balawyder, In the Clutches of the Kremlin, 115
10. Balawyder, On the Road to Freedom, 99
11. Hansard May 14 1951, 3003
12. Hansard May 5 1953, 4829; Balawyder, In the Clutches of the Kremlin, 126
13. Warnock, Partner to Behemoth, 28
14. Pearson, Memoirs 2, 40
15. Bercuson, Canada and the Birth of Israel, 140; English, The Worldly Years, 12
16. Robinson, Pearson Phenomenon, 95
17. Reid, Radical Mandarin, 252
18. Beal, Pearson of Canada, 96
19. MacMillan, Canada and NATO, 44
20. Warnock, Partner to Behemoth, 65
21. Warnock, Partner to Behemoth, 65
22. Cardwell, NSC 68, 38
23. Bothwell, Alliance and Illusion, 46
24. Chomsky, What Uncle Sam Really Wants, 78
25. Cardwell, NSC 68, 51
26. Roberts Wayne, Canadian Dimension June 1981
27. Roberts Wayne Canadian Dimension June 1981; Warnock John, Canadian Dimension Mar 1973
28. Hansard Nov 16 1949, 1840
29. Gonick, Inflation or Depression, 231
30. Jervis, The Meaning of the Nuclear Revolution, 207
31. Hansard Mar 28 1949, 2095

Lester Pearson's Peacekeeping

32. Pearson, Memoirs 2, 47
33. http://en.wikipedia.org/wiki/Operation_Gladio
34. Gasner, NATO's Secret Armies, 2
35. Gasner, NATO's Secret Armies, 26
36. http://www.cbc.ca/news/canada/montreal/story/2010/10/13/profunc-canadian-communist-blacklist.html
37. Hansard Feb 4 1949, 237
38. Hansard Oct 19 1951, 196
39. Hansard Feb 11 1953, 1855
40. Hansard Oct 22 1951, 254
41. Price, Orienting Canada, 282
42. Hansard May 5 1953, 4832
43. Hansard Apr 1 1952, 1014
44. Bercuson, Blood on the Hills, 29
45. Eayrs, Northern Approaches, 61
46. Stairs, Diplomacy of Constraint, 173
47. Munton, Canadian Foreign Policy: selected cases, 2
48. Bercuson, Blood on the Hill, 32
49. Price, Orienting Canada, 304
50. Bercuson, Canada and the Birth of Israel, 33
51. Bercuson, Canada and the Birth of Israel, 68; Tauber, Personal Policy Making, 3
52. Bercuson, Canada and the Birth of Israel, 70
53. Bercuson, Canada and the Birth of Israel, 72
54. Bercuson, Canada and the Birth of Israel, 73
55. Kaplan, Canadian Maverick, 230
56. Tauber, Personal Policymaking, 8
57. Tauber, Personal Policymaking, 8
58. Bercuson, Canada and the Birth of Israel, 138
59. Khalidi Walid, www.palestinestudies.org: Revisiting the UNGA Partition Resolution
60. Kay, Canada and Palestine, 134
61. Kay, Canada and Palestine, 137
62. Taras, Domestic Battleground, 129
63. Taras, Domestic Battleground, 136
64. Tauber, Personal Policy Making, 78 & 82
65. Tauber, Personal Policy Making, 86
66. Halifax Chronicle-Herald Nov 20 2001; Heinbecker, Canada and the Middle East, 10
67. Pappe, Ethnic Cleansing of Palestine, 29
68. Pappe, Ethnic Cleansing of Palestine, 18
69. Pappe, Ethnic Cleansing of Palestine, 34
70. Tauber, Personal Policy Making, 32
71. Tauber, Personal Policy Making, 94
72. Tauber, Personal Policy Making, 91
73. Andrew, The Rise and Fall of a Middle Power, 79
74. Kay, Canada and Palestine, 123
75. Pappe, The Ethnic Cleansing of Palestine, 35
76. Khalidi, The Iron Cage, 1
77. Morris, 1948, 181
78. Kay, Canada and Palestine, 152
79. Bercuson, Canada and the Birth of Israel, 209
80. Heinbecker, Canada and the Middle East, 12
81. Hilāl, Canadian Foreign Policy and the Palestine Problem, 13
82. Hull, The Fall and Rise of Israel, 383
83. Kay, Canada and Palestine, 2
84. Kay, Canada and Palestine, 160
85. Tauber, Personal Policy Making, 84
86. Stursberg, Lester Pearson and the American dilemma, X
87. Pearson, Four Faces of Peace, 23
88. Abella, None is Too Many, 205
89. Abella, None is Too Many, 136
90. Tauber, Personal Policy Making, 85
91. Anderson, Pearson and the myth of neutrality, Toronto Star Nov 5 2006
92. Tauber, Personal Policy Making, 81
93. Tauber, Personal Policy Making, 30
94. Tauber, Personal Policy Making, 30
95. Taras, The Domestic Battleground, 31/137
96. Bristman, In the Strategic Interests of Canada, 52
97. Bristman, In the Strategic Interests of Canada, 52
98. Pearson, Memoirs 2, 219

Chapter 3

1. Price, Contradictory impulses, 135
2. Austin, Saving China, 290; Bothwell, Alliance and Illusion, 32; Evans, Reluctant Adversaries, 29
3. Gimblett, Canadian Gunboat Diplomacy, 90
4. Lee, Outposts of Empire, 59
5. Hansard Nov 16 1949, 1838
6. Hansard Jan 31 1956, 710; Hansard Mar 24 1955, 2337
7. Hansard June 15 1951, 4194; Hansard June 6 1951, 3771
8. Chomsky, Deterring Democracy, 124
9. Peck, Washington's China, 227
10. LeVos, The war for men's minds, 36
11. Gendron, Towards a Francophone Community, 24
12. Price, Orienting Canada, 180
13. Chomsky, What Uncle Sam really wants, 111
14. Wood, Strange Battleground, 6
15. Stairs, Diplomacy of Constraint, 15
16. Stairs, Diplomacy of Constraint, 17
17. Stairs, Diplomacy of Constraint, 15
18. Pearson, Memoirs 2, 140
19. Smith, Diplomacy of Fear, 217
20. Pearson, Memoirs 2, 143
21. Stairs, Diplomacy of Constraint, 13
22. Stairs, Diplomacy of Constraint, 15
23. Smith, Diplomacy of Fear, 217
24. Price, Orienting Canada, 183
25. Stairs, Diplomacy of Constraint, 205
26. Stairs, Diplomacy of Constraint, 27
27. Hansard Aug 31 1950, 92; Stairs, Diplomacy of Constraint, 25
28. Price, Orienting Canada, 190
29. Hart-Landsberg, Korea, 121
30. McKercher, North Atlantic Triangle in a Changing World, 223
31. Hansard June 28 1950, 4251
32. McKercher, North Atlantic Triangle in a Changing World, 223
33. Blum, Killing Hope, 49
34. Blum, Killing Hope, 49
35. Stairs, Diplomacy of Constraint, 205
36. Taylor, Tested Mettle 10
37. Pearson, Memoirs 2, 149
38. Bercuson, True Patriot, 210
39. The Worldly Years, 49
40. Taylor, Tested Mettle, 11
41. Hart-Landsberg, Korea, 133
42. Price, Orienting Canada, 270
43. Stone, The Hidden History of the Korean War, 258
44. Price, Orienting Canada, 271
45. Whitaker, Cold War Canada, 391
46. Hansard May 14 1951, 3013
47. Wood, Strange Battleground, 197
48. Watson, Far Eastern Tour, 82
49. Watson, Far Eastern Tour, 90
50. Watson, Far Eastern Tour, 15
51. Madsen, Another Kind of Justice, 110
52. Bercuson, Blood on the Hills, 177
53. English, The Worldly Years, 29
54. Hansard Sep 4 1950, 230
55. Peck, Washington's China, 156
56. Cardwell, NSC 68, 210; Chomsky, Necessary Illusions, 29
57. Whitaker, Cold War Canada, 392
58. Cardwell, NSC 68, 18
59. Hansard Sep 1 1950, 111
60. Hansard Aug 31 1950, 95
61. Stairs, Diplomacy of Constraint, 332
62. Stairs, Diplomacy of Constraint, 104
63. Watson, Far Eastern Tour, 32
64. Chapnick, Canada's Voice, 71
65. Canadian Foreign Policy, 305
66. Stone, The Hidden History of the Korean War, 171
67. English, The Worldly Years, 55
68. Stursberg, Lester Person and the American Dilemma, 89
69. Pearson, Memoirs 2, 170
70. Pearson, Memoirs 2, 308
71. Pearson, Memoirs 2, 308
72. Hansard Mar 24 1955, 2343
73. Price, Contradictory Impulses, 135
74. Price, Contradictory Impulses, 133
75. Price, Contradictory Impulses, 5
76. Price, Contradictory Impulses, 135

Lester Pearson's Peacekeeping

77. Price, Contradictory Impulses, 135
78. Price, Contradictory Impulses, 127
79. Price, Orienting Canada, 172
80. Price, Orienting Canada, 143; Orienting Canada, 189
81. Price, Contradictory Impulses, 128
82. Chomsky, At War with Asia, 9
83. Price, Contradictory Impulses 129
84. Price, Contradictory Impulses, 5
85. Price, Orienting Canada, 187
86. Hansard Feb 11 1953, 1855; Hansard Feb 22 1950, 131
87. Hansard Aug 31 1950, 94
88. Hansard June 20 1952, 3502
89. http://en.wikipedia.org/wiki/Gerald_Templer
90. http://en.wikipedia.org/wiki/Malayan_Emergency
91. http://www.newworldencyclopedia.org/entry/Indonesian_War_of_Independence
92. Webster, Fire and the Full Moon, 35
93. Webster, Fire and the Full Moon, 38
94. Webster, Fire and the full moon, 16
95. Webster, Fire and the Full Moon, 40
96. Webster, Fire and the Full Moon, 35
97. Webster, Fire and the Full Moon, 34
98. Webster, Fire and the Full Moon, 38
99. Webster, Fire and the Full Moon, 105
100. Webster, Fire and Full Moon, 105
101. Chomsky, the Washington Connection, 300
102. Lee, Outposts of Empire, 57
103. Hansard Feb 22 1950,133
104. Chomsky, Studies in Political Economy, 1985
105. Chomsky, http://canadiandimension.com/articles/3217
106. Lee, Outposts of Empire, 228
107. Hansard May 10 1954, 4547
108. Warnock, Partner to Behemoth, 80
109. Levant, Quiet Complicity, 44
110. Price, Orienting Canada, 282
111. Levant, Quiet Complicity, 43
112. Gendron, Towards a Francophone Community, 31
113. Zinn, A People's History of the United States, 471
114. English, The Worldly Years, 91
115. Price, Orienting Canada, 298
116. Levant, Quiet Complicity, 129
117. Blum, Killing Hope, 126
118. Hansard Aug 2 1956, 6880
119. Levant, Quiet Complicity, 127
120. Levant, Quiet Complicity, 128
121. Levant, Quiet Complicity, 133
122. Levant, Quiet Complicity, 193
123. Gafuik, More Than a Peacemaker, 40
124. Webster, Fire and Full Moon, 52
125. Shaw, Grudging Gifts
126. Carty, Perpetuating Poverty, 45
127. Hansard Aug 2 1956, 6866
128. Hansard Aug 1 1956, 6834
129. Hansard Aug 1 1956, 6834

Chapter 4

1. Regehr, Arms Canada, 39
2. External Affairs file 50152 - 40 - 55 volume 5859
3. Kinzer, All the Shah's Men, 80
4. Kinzer, All the Shah's Men, 80
5. Kinzer, All the Shah's Men, 87
6. Hansard May 14 1951, 3002
7. Hansard Oct 22 1951, 253
8. Netherton, In/Security, 345
9. Kinzer, All the Shah's Men, 160
10. Kinzer, All the Shah's Men, 160
11. External Affairs file 50152 - 40 - 31 Vol. 5859
12. External Affairs file 50152 - 40 - 42 Vol. 5859
13. External Affairs file 50152 - 40 - 42 Vol. 5859
14. External Affairs file 50152 - 40 - 31 Vol. 5859
15. http://en.wikipedia.org/wiki/Foreign_relations_of_Canada
16. Schlesinger, Bitter Fruit, 75
17. Schlesinger, Bitter Fruit, 12
18. Schlesinger, Bitter Fruit, 73
19. Chomsky, Year 501, 37

Lester Pearson's Peacekeeping

20. http://en.wikipedia.org/wiki/1954_Guatemalan_coup_d%27%C3%A9tat
21. McFarlane, Northern Shadows, 99
22. McFarlane, Northern Shadows, 99
23. McFarlane, Northern Shadows 98
24. Rochlin, Discovering the Americas, 35
25. McFarlane, Northern Shadows, 100
26. http://search.beaconforfreedom.org/about_database/south%20africa.html
27. http://www.globalsecurity.org/military/world/war/south_africa1.htm
28. Freeman, Ambiguous Champion, 17
29. Hansard Dec 8 1949, 2924
30. Freeman, Ambiguous Champion, 17
31. Tennyson, Canadian Relations with South Africa, 139
32. Tennyson, Canadian Relations with South Africa, 136
33. Freeman, Ambiguous Champion, 16
34. Hansard Feb 12 1953, 1865; Hansard Jan 14 1957, 179
35. Hansard Jan 14 1957, 175
36. Hansard Feb 7 1956, 942
37. Gendron, Towards a Francophone Community, 23
38. Gendron, Towards a Francophone Community, 35
39. Gendron, Towards a Francophone Community, 36
40. http://en.wikipedia.org/wiki/Torture_during_the_Algerian_War
41. Gendron, Towards a Francophone Community, 17
42. Hansard Mar 28 1949, 2099
43. Gendron, Towards a Francophone Community, 32
44. Gendron, Towards a Francophone community, 41
45. Gendron, Towards a Francophone Community, 28
46. Gendron, Towards a Francophone Community, 38
47. Gendron, Towards a Francophone Community, 28
48. Hansard Oct 19 1951, 196
49. Delvoie, Canada and Egypt, 1
50. Delvoie, Canada and Egypt, 2
51. Bristman, In the Strategic Interests of Canada, 150
52. Bristman, In the Strategic Interests of Canada, 39
53. Bristman, In the Strategic Interests of Canada, 52
54. Bristman, In the Strategic Interests of Canada, 133
55. Pearson, Seize the Day, 147
56. http://en.wikipedia.org/wiki/Suez_Crisis
57. Carroll, Pearson's Peacekeepers, 23
58. McQuaig, Holding the Bully's Coat, 155
59. Pearson, Seize the Day, 157
60. Rosner, United Nations Emergency Force, 23
61. Thordarson, Lester Pearson: Diplomat and Politician, 86
62. Lyon, Canada and the Third World, 249
63. Thomson, Louis St. Laurent, 475
64. Blanchette, Canadian Foreign Policy: 1945-2000, 39
65. Pearson, Seize the Day, 147
66. Ismael, Canadian-Arab Relations, 17
67. Carroll, Pearson's Peacekeepers, 8
68. Hansard Aug 1 1956, 6831
69. Delvoie, Canada and Egypt, 3
70. Carroll, Pearson's Peacekeepers, 13
71. Carroll, Pearson's Peacekeepers, 16
72. Taylor, Peacekeeping, 45
73. Maloney, Canada and U.N. Peacekeeping, 69; Starnes, Closely Guarded, 119
74. Gafuik, More Than a Peacemaker, 80
75. Hansard Mar 15 1957, 2361/2362
76. Rosner, United Nations Emergency Force, 31; Thomson, Louis St. Laurent, 481
77. Taylor, Peacekeeping, 129
78. Delvoie, Canada and Egypt, 19
79. Carroll, Pearson's Peacekeepers, 35
80. Hansard Mar 7 1957, 1959
81. Eayrs, The Commonwealth and Suez, 342
82. Rosner, United Nations Emergency Force, 137
83. Harbottle, The Blue Berets, 11

Lester Pearson's Peacekeeping

84. Eayrs, The Commonwealth and Suez, 430
85. Bernard Avishai, Nation Jul 6 2009
86. Rosner, United Nations Emergency Force, 75
87. Dessouki, Canadian Foreign Policy and the Palestine Problem, 27
88. Dessouki, Canadian Foreign Policy and the Palestine Problem, 27

Chapter 5

1. Finch, Exporting Danger, 37
2. Clearwater, Canadian Nuclear Weapons, 18
3. Clearwater, Just Dummies, 208
4. Finch, Exporting Danger, 34
5. Maloney, Canada and UN Peacekeeping, 123; Levitt, Pearson and Canada's Role in Nuclear Disarmament, 69
6. Maloney, Canada and UN Peacekeeping, 53
7. Levitt, Pearson and Canada's Role in Nuclear Disarmament, 168
8. Levitt, Pearson and Canada's Role in Nuclear Disarmament, 69 & 284
9. Levitt, Pearson and Canada's Role in Nuclear Disarmament, 206
10. Levitt, Pearson and Canada's Role in Nuclear Disarmament, 215
11. Levitt, Pearson and Canada's Role in Nuclear Disarmament, 283
12. Levitt, Pearson and Canada's Role in Nuclear Disarmament, 170
13. Levitt, Pearson and Canada's Role in Nuclear Disarmament, 140
14. Levitt, Pearson and Canada's Role in Nuclear Disarmament, 141
15. Clearwater, Canadian Nuclear Weapons, 185
16. Clearwater, Canadian Nuclear Weapons, 214
17. Clearwater, Canadian Nuclear Weapons, 123
18. Levitt, Pearson and Canada's Role in Nuclear Disarmament, 67
19. Whitaker, Cold War Canada, 373
20. Whitaker, Cold War Canada, 375
21. Nash, Kennedy and Diefenbaker, 201
22. Haydon, The 1962 Cuban Missile Crisis, 33
23. Haydon, The 1962 Cuban Missile Crisis, 113
24. Reford, Canada and three crises, 190
25. Nash, Kennedy and Diefenbaker, 214
26. Nash, Kennedy and Diefenbaker 281
27. Nash, Kennedy and Diefenbaker, 15
28. Nash, Kennedy and Diefenbaker, 90
29. McFarlane, Northern Shadows, 114
30. Stursberg, Lester Pearson and the American Dilemma, 183
31. McFarlane, Northern Shadows, 115
32. McFarlane, Northern Shadows, 115
33. Stursberg, Lester Person and the American Dilemma, 181
34. Stursberg, Lester Pearson and the American Dilemma, 185
35. Nash, Diefenbaker and Kennedy, 166
36. Stursberg, Lester Pearson and the American dilemma, 187
37. Clearwater, US Nuclear Weapons in Canada, 84
38. Clearwater, Canadian Nuclear Weapons, 93/94
39. Clearwater, Canadian Nuclear Weapons, 27
40. Clearwater, Canadian Nuclear Weapons, 64

Chapter 6

1. Kirk, Canada-Cuba Relations, 66
2. Kirk, Canada-Cuba Relations, 83
3. Kirk, Canada-Cuba Relations, 84
4. Kirk, Canada-Cuba Relations, 82
5. Kirk, Canada-Cuba Relations, 67
6. McFarlane, Northern Shadows, 116
7. Hansard Nov 14 1963, 4718
8. http://en.wikipedia.org/wiki/CIA_activities_in_Brazil
9. Barbosa, Brazil and Canada in the Americas, 44
10. Latin America Working Group Letter Vol iv #2
11. Last Post Mar 1973 Vol 3 #2

12. Last Post Mar 1973 Vol 3 #2
13. Arruda, The Multinational Corporations and Brazil, 94
14. Latin America Working Group Letter Vol iv #2
15. Latin America Working Group Letter Vol iv #2
16. Last Post Mar 1973 Vol 3 #2
17. Chodos, Let us Prey, 17
18. Latin America Working Group Letter Vol 11 #8
19. Hansard May 3 1965, 831
20. Hansard May 21 1965, 1560
21. Hansard May 11 1965, 1152
22. Hansard May 4 1965, 887
23. Hansard May 28 1965, 1777
24. Carty, Perpetuating Poverty, 64; Latin America Working Group Letter Vol 3 #4
25. Hansard Apr 29 1965, 721
26. Latin America Working Group Letter Vol 11 #8
27. Wright, Our Place in the Sun, 136
28. Wright, Our Place in the Sun, 135
29. Gimblett, Canadian Gunboat Diplomacy, 153
30. Smillie, Land of Lost Content, 35
31. Winks, Canadian-West Indian Union, 42
32. Freeman, Ambiguous Champion, 22
33. http://www.fotim.ac.za/fotim_conferences/genderconf/papers/lane_paper.pdf
34. Hansard June 14 1964, 4179
35. Freeman, Ambiguous Champion, 47
36. Freeman, Ambiguous Champion, 29
37. Hansard Oct 31 1963, 4213
38. Hansard Nov 14 1963, 4726
39. Hansard Nov 28 1963, 5199
40. Freeman, Ambiguous Champion, 34
41. Freeman, Ambiguous Champion, 33
42. Freeman, Ambiguous Champion, 32
43. Freeman, Ambiguous Champion, 32
44. Freeman, Ambiguous Champion, 31
45. Words and Deeds, 8
46. Words and Deeds, 12
47. External Affairs file 20 - 13 - 3 - Portugal - 19 - RG 25 volume 9318
48. External Affairs file 20 - 13 - 3 - Portugal - 15
49. External Affairs file 20 - 13 - 3 - Portugal - 25
50. Words and Deeds, 65
51. Words and Deeds, 68
52. http://www.seeingblack.com/x060702/nkrumah.shtml
53. Schlegel, The Deceptive Ash, 63
54. Howell, Ghana and Nkrumah, 129/143
55. Howell, Ghana and Nkrumah, 149
56. Schlegel, The Deceptive Ash, 64
57. Hansard Mar 17 1966, 2808
58. Canadian Institute for International Affairs Vol V #3
59. Howell, Ghana and Nkrumah, 175
60. Hansard May 24 1967, 531
61. Hansard May 26 1967, 601
62. Dewitt, Canada as a Principle Power, 382; Ismael, Canadian-Arab Relations, 10; Taylor, Peacekeeping, 140
63. Hansard May 24 1967, 532
64. Finkelstein, Image and Reality of the Israel-Palestine Conflict, 138
65. Finkelstein, Image and Reality of the Israel-Palestine Conflict, 143
66. Hansard June 5 1967, 1134
67. Hansard June 8 1967, 1294
68. Hansard June 8 1967, 1321
69. Kay, Diplomacy of Impartiality, 60
70. Hansard June 16 1967, 1595
71. Dessouki, Canadian Foreign Policy and the Palestine Problem, 40
72. Gordon, Israel's Occupation, 6; Said, The End of the Peace Process, 270
73. Hansard June 16 1967, 1596
74. Gordon, Israel's Occupation, 6; Said, The End of the Peace Process, 270

Chapter 7

1. http://www.duhaime.org/LegalDictionary/W/WarCrimes.aspx
2. Webster, Fire and Full Moon, 142
3. Webster, Fire and the Full Moon, 191
4. Webster, Fire and the Full Moon, 149

Lester Pearson's Peacekeeping

5. Webster, Fire and the Full Moon, 150
6. Webster, Fire and the Full Moon, 150
7. Webster, Fire and Full Moon, 141
8. Webster, Fire and Full Moon, 137
9. http://en.wikipedia.org/wiki/Indonesian_killings_of_1965%E2%80%931966
10. Webster, Fire and Full Moon, 152
11. Webster, Fire and the full moon, 153
12. Webster, Fire and the Full Moon, 154
13. Morrison, Aid and Ebb Tide, 74
14. Nossal, Rain Dancing, 39
15. Webster, Fire and Full Moon, 151
16. Webster, Fire and Full Moon, 155
17. http://en.wikipedia.org/wiki/Vietnam_War
18. Chomsky, At War with Asia, 88
19. http://en.wikipedia.org/wiki/My_Lai_Massacre
20. http://hnn.us/articles/1802.html
21. http://en.wikipedia.org/wiki/Phoenix_Program
22. Zinn, A People's History of the United States, 478
23. Warnock, Partner to Behemoth, 285
24. Hansard Apr 26 1965, 399
25. Hansard Apr 6 1965, 11
26. Hansard Feb 16 1965, 11372
27. Hansard May 24 1967, 529
28. Levant, Quiet Complicity, 48
29. McQuaig, Holding the Bully's Coat, 145
30. Strusberg, Lester Pearson and the American Dilemma, 254
31. Levant, Quiet Complicity, 197
32. English, The Worldly Years, 366
33. Pearson, Memoirs 3, 142
34. Hansard Jan 31 1966, 431
35. Hansard June 29 1966, 7018
36. Hansard April 21, 15180
37. Hillmer, Pearson: the Unlikely Gladiator, 148
38. Levant, Quiet Complicity, 8
39. Levant, Quiet Complicity, 4
40. Levant, Quiet Complicity, 82
41. Levant, Quiet Complicity, 73
42. Hansard Oct 11 1967, 2980
43. Regehr, Arms Canada, 61
44. Regehr, Making a Killing, 3; Levant, Quiet Complicity, 4; Chomsky, Understanding Power, 290
45. Taylor, Snow Job, 121
46. Levant, Quiet Complicity, 57
47. Levant, Quiet Complicity, 57
48. Regehr, Making a Killing, 8
49. Hansard Feb 3 1967, 12614
50. Regehr, Arms Canada, 48
51. Taylor, Snow Job, 122
52. Levant, Quiet Complicity, 204-205
53. Levant, Quiet Complicity, 205
54. Gaffen, Unknown Warriors, 33
55. Levant, Quiet Complicity, 203
56. Chomsky, The Washington Connection, 321
57. Levant, Quiet Complicity, 108
58. Warnock, Partner to Behemoth 285
59. Levant, Quiet Complicity, 195
60. Taylor, Snow Job, 18
61. Levant, Quiet Complicity, 196
62. Taylor, Snow Job, 57
63. Taylor, Snow Job, 57
64. Strusberg, Lester Pearson and the American Dilemma, 256
65. Taylor, Snow Job, 51
66. Strusberg, Lester Pearson and the American dilemma, 258
67. Taylor, Snow Job, 84
68. http://www.vietnamwar.net/quotations/quotations.htm
69. Chomsky, American Power, 15

Chapter 8

1. Azzi, Walter Gordon and the rise of Canadian Nationalism, 27
2. English, Shadows of Heaven, 279
3. Thordarson, Lester Pearson: diplomat and politician, 39
4. Cohen, Lester B. Pearson, 76
5. Maloney, Canada and UN Peacekeeping, 29
6. Tennyson, Canadian Relations with South Africa, 116
7. Chapnick, Canada's Voice, 108
8. McQuaig, Holding the Bully's Coat, 150

9. Cardwell, NSC 68, 26
10. Hansard May 20 1963, 62
11. Gellner, Canada and NATO, 48
12. Strusberg, Lester Pearson and the American Dilemma, 309
13. Beal, Pearson of Canada, 96
14. Hansard Jan 29 1954, 1587
15. McQuaig, Holding Bully's Coat, 146
16. Thakur, Peacekeeping in Vietnam, 8
17. Pearson, Memoirs, 284
18. Stairs, In the National Interest, 143
19. Warnock, Partner to Behemoth, 63; Canadian Dimension Mar 1973
20. Strusberg, Lester Person and the American Dilemma, 179
21. Clement, Continental Corporate Power, 179
22. Chodos, Let us Prey, 28
23. Price, Orienting Canada, 12; In the National Interest, 88
24. Price, Orienting Canada, 229
25. English, The Worldly Years, 393
26. Strusberg, Lester Pearson and the American Dilemma, 239; Cohen, Lester B. Pearson, 103
27. English, The Worldly Years, 66
28. Azzi, Walter Gordon and the rise of Canadian Nationalism, 28
29. Azzi, Walter Gordon and the rise of Canadian Nationalism, 28
30. http://journalism.ukings.ca/journalism_3719.html
31. http://archives.cbc.ca/economy_business/the_media/clips/4832/
32. Hansard Apr 6 1955, 2885
33. Chapnick, Canada's Voice, 25
34. Chapnick, Canada's Voice, 193
35. Cohen, Lester B. Pearson, 102
36. Hansard Nov 17 1949, 1924
37. Wood, Strange Battleground, 12
38. Levitt, Pearson and Canada's Role in Nuclear Disarmament, 82
39. Holmes, The Shaping of Peace Vol. 2, 120
40. Pearson, Words and Occasions, 126
41. Pearson, Words and Occasions, 124
42. Pearson, Words and Occasions, 81
43. McQaig, Holding the Bully's Coat, 150
44. http://www.iciss.ca/report2-en.asp
45. The Lancet Oct 11 2006; iraqbodycount.org
46. http://www.canadahaitiaction.ca/
47. Kolbe Athena, Lancet Sep 2 2006
48. Pearson, Four Faces of Peace, 242

Praise for Stop Signs — Cars and Capitalism

"Probably the most comprehensive assessment of the power of the automobile... Stop Signs is a powerful tool for raising awareness of the multiple and self-reinforcing ways automotivism dominates us." *Carbusters*

"The accumulation of arguments starts to feel persuasive. You question whether your own auto-programming has blinded you." *Toronto Star*

"A stocking stuffer that might possibly reform, or more likely honk off, your favorite gas-guzzling SUV owner." *Chicago Tribune*

"Smart and expansive critique of car-dependent North America that is convincing and frightening. This book is an eye-opener for everyone — from the stubborn car-lover to the anti-car activist who wants to brush up on the facts." *Montréal Review of Books*

"Stop Signs takes the myriad problems associated with a world obsessed with cars and wraps them up in a concise, compelling, and at times even funny, plea to quit the automobile." *Canadian Dimension*

"A key read for anyone looking to gain knowledge and insight into the contemporary crossroads faced by societies increasingly dependant and shaped by the automobile. Although factually and footnote heavy, it's an engaging and quick read." *Rabble.ca*

"Stop Signs is a riveting read on the perniciousness and the falsities that undergird car culture." *Dissidentvoice.org*

"Each city visited opens up a fact-filled reflection on the social, cultural, economic, and environmental destructiveness of automobility .... this book could not be more relevant." *Syracuse Peace Council Newsletter*

"More than the sum of its impressive array of facts. It's a journey, a tale, a wallow, and it has its poetry and pleasures. ... Good stuff. Buy it, steal it, or—as I did—beg for it." *Counterpunch.org*

Praise for Canada and Israel: Building Apartheid

"The only book that need be written on Canada's policies towards Israel... The most carefully documented book relating to the Israel/Palestine conflict I have ever read." *Michael Neumann, author of The Case Against Israel, CounterPunch.org*

"Engler's style is clear and direct. He writes with passion and careful documentation." *London Free Press*

"Excellent little book ... should be mandatory to be read by the politicians of the country." *Pacific Free Press*

"Skillfully constructs a coherent narrative ... well-referenced and easy-to-follow exposé." *Electronic Intifada*

"Fortunately, there are still publishers that will take on writers like Engler." *Canadian Dimension*

"Comprehensive... easy-to-read." *Toronto Now*

"Indispensable resource for students and activists alike." *New Socialist*

"Fine work." *Zmag.org*

"Eminently eloquent document that needs to be read for its well-researched position." *Montréal Serai*

"Contains much essential information." *Dissidentvoice.org*

"For a country that prides itself on its commitment to goodness (and its opposition to imperialism), the book's challenge is potentially transformative." *Journal of Palestine Studies*

"Everyone interested in furthering human rights and undermining imperialism at home and abroad should read this book." *Socialist Worker*

"Masterfull." *L'aut'journal*

"Cleverly brings together history, information, and fact in easy narrative." *Muslimlink.ca*

"Concise and informative history of Canada's foreign policy towards Israel ... an important and timely book." *Socialist Studies*

"A stunning examination of the history of Canada-Israel relations and a key read for anyone interested in Canadian foreign policy." *Montréal Hour*

Praise for Black Book of Canadian Foreign Policy

"A must-read." *Halifax Chronicle Herald*

"Leftist gadfly tears down foreign policy." *Ottawa Citizen*

"Best critical survey of Canadian foreign policy to date." *Upping the Anti*

"Encyclopedic look at Canadian misdeeds." *Toronto Now*

"The best gift I could have hoped for as I retired after 35 years as a foreign affairs journalist with [Montréal daily] La Presse." *Jooneed Khan, Montréal Serai*

"Broad in scope and packing many a punch, The Black Book of Canadian Foreign Policy is likely to become an important reference for international solidarity activists." *Montreal Hour*

"Engler presents an impressive cascade of evidence that Canada is not exactly a force for good in the world." *Montréal Review of Books*

"A book that has been desperately needed for a long time." *New Socialist*

"Persuasive, well researched, sweeping historical critique of Canadian foreign policy." *People's Voice*

"Whatever your politics, it's hard to put down The Black Book without seriously questioning Canada's image." *Concordia Link*

"An extremely interesting and quite largely convincing book." *Rabble.ca*

"Fine book." *Socialist Worker*

"Marshals a wealth of evidence to show that the state consistently represents Canada's business elite." *Labour/Le Travail*

"Lays out the facts on Canada's sinister role as a partner in world imperialist and colonial quests." *Canadian Charger*

"Engler's book is written in a concise, straightforward style that mostly lets the meticulously referenced facts speak for themselves." *Zmag.org*

"One of the most important studies of Canada's international role in years." *Briarpatch magazine*